And he saw also a certain poor widow....

Luke 21:2

i

ii

RUTH

A Living Parable of Jesus Christ

Contents

Preface 1

Introduction 3

    About the Book of Ruth 4

    Searching for Jesus 5

    Parable 6

    Living Parables 7

    The Name of God 9

    GOEL 11

    GOEL - The Kinsman-Redeemer 12

    Introduction to the Story 13

Chapter 1 14

    The Famine 15

    And the Woman was Left 18

    The War 21

    The Living Parable 24

    The Hearing Ear 27

    The Name of God 29

    The Kiss 32

    The Living Sacrifice 35

    The Helper 37

    Call Me Mara 39

Chapter 2 42

And His Name was Boaz.. 43

God's Provision 45

Gleaning after the Reapers 47

Strength Came from Bethlehem............................... 50

God with Us 52

Whose damsel is this? 55

Meeting Ruth... 58

Hearest Thou Not? 60

She Fell Down 62

The Broken Wall... 65

After the Death... 68

His Name's Sake 70

Comforted... 72

The Master's Table 74

Handfuls on Purpose.. 76

An Ephah of Barley 79

The Unveiling Word.. 81

The Dead 84

Not My Will 86

Chapter 3 89

Seeking Rest 90

Naomi's Turn... 93

The Feet of the Redeemer 96

Ruth's Response 101

She Went Down.. 104

Entering into His Rest 106

A Woman Rejected 108

The Power of Love 112

Losing Life, and Finding It....................................116

Tarrying at His Feet... 120

The Secret 122

Waiting for the Redeemer.................................... 124

Chapter 4 126

Boaz Prevails...127

The Sandal.. 132

Day of Redemption 136

The Seed of the Woman.......................................138

The New Birth 141

The Virtuous Woman..143

Restorer of Life... 145

The Day of Small Things......................................147

The Coming King.. 150

The Assembly of the LORD 153

Appendix... 155

On the Use of Multiple Translations................... 156

Meanings of the Names 157

On Ruth's Desire to Work with the Young Men.................. 158

On uncovering the feet of Boaz 159

About Hiram.. 160

On the Pillar named Jachin.....................................161

Tamar.. 162

Resources 169

Preface

1st Peter 2:21 For even hereunto were ye called: because Christ also suffered for us, leaving us an example ….

The amazing thing is that without Christ, none of the imagery found in this story could ever be seen. It simply would not be there. It is only through the advent of Jesus Christ, including His suffering and death, that the narrative of this family and the devastation they experienced gains meaning that looks beyond the grave, and reaches above the skies.

Without the cross, I would never have experienced the grace of God to be able to see what is there, and share it with you. And even knowing Him, it took suffering and loss even on our part. In April of 1991, my wife Sarah and I lost our five-year-old son, Jeremy. We entrusted someone to watch over him while we were away for a day, and he drowned in a river. We know devastation personally; not a friend, but part of all things.

Romans 8:28 And we know that all things work together for good to them that love God, to them who are the called according to his purpose.

So we have these four small chapters; this historical narrative showing us the greatness of God, who is continually working all things for *our* good, even when *we* would long for death. In this process of being conformed into His likeness, we must learn that suffering is part of who He is. And we are to be *like* Him.

1

Romans 8:18 For I reckon that the sufferings of this present time are not worthy to be compared with the glory which shall be revealed in us.

J. C. Farris

Introduction

About the Book of Ruth

As the story begins, *in the days when the judges ruled*, the book of Ruth is placed appropriately after the book of Judges, and in front of 1st Samuel. It bridges the gap from the time of the judges to the days when kings ruled in Israel, with the genealogy at the end of Ruth providing the lineage to King David.

No one knows who wrote the book of Ruth, though tradition credits Samuel for its composition, as he was the prophet who anointed David to be king over Israel (1st Samuel 16:1-13). The common practice of kingdoms to keep genealogical records of their kings dates back to the beginning of recorded history. As Ruth is the earliest source for David's genealogy in the Bible, it was likely written during David's reign, around 1000 B. C.

Searching for Jesus

John 5:39 You search the Scriptures, for in them you think you have eternal life; and these are they which testify of Me. (NKJV)

Whenever we are searching for someone, it helps to know some things about that person. So in order to *see* Jesus as we read the Scriptures (the Old Testament), we need to know some things about Him. It is good to have some knowledge of the gospel narratives (Matthew, Mark, Luke and John), which record His actions and teachings, and reveal Him as the Son of God who died on the cross for our sins, and was resurrected on the third day. It also helps to be familiar with the letters of the New Testament (or epistles, as they are properly called), as they explain what Jesus accomplished on the cross; why the cross was necessary; His resurrection, ascension, the sending of the Holy Spirit, and what He is doing now through the power of His Spirit. They also provide us with information on such things as baptism, redemption, grace, intercession, the work of the Holy Spirit, and many other details that help us understand more fully what Jesus is all about.

When we know these things, we can begin to see the parallels to Jesus as they appear throughout the Old Testament, and particularly here in the book of Ruth. Having this understanding enables us to grasp the message beyond the story; this living parable of Jesus Christ.

Parable

παραβολή

parabolē

1) a placing of one thing by the side of another, juxtaposition, as of ships in battle

2) metaphorically

    2a) a comparing, comparison of one thing with another, likeness, similitude

    2b) an example by which a doctrine or precept is illustrated

- Thayer's Greek Lexicon of the New Testament

_____

Living Parables

... I do nothing of myself; but as my Father hath taught me, I speak these things.

John 8:28

Jesus taught using parables. He used earthly illustrations to help people understand things about God and His kingdom. He told stories of situations that people were familiar with; things that actually happened in everyday life. In that sense, the stories He told were true. A woman did look for a coin (Luke 15:8-10). A man did wait for his son (Luke 15:11-32). A king did hold a feast (Matthew 22:1-14).

By teaching in parables, Jesus was not doing anything new, for God had already been speaking this way to us throughout the Old Testament. When Jesus speaks in parables, it simply shows that He takes after His Father.

In analyzing the narratives of the Old Testament, it is not difficult to find similarities in them to the life and work of Christ. Biblical scholars call these similarities, *types*. There are *types* of Christ found in the stories of Joseph and Moses, for example. As these stories *pair well* with the message of the gospel, I prefer to call them, *living parables*. They are parables of recorded history, and there are many of them. Jesus shared some of them during His time here on earth; like this one, which He shared with a man named Nicodemus:

John 3:14 And as Moses lifted up the serpent in the wilderness, even so must the Son of man be lifted up:
3:15 That whosoever believeth in him should not perish, but have eternal life.

Jesus spoke of the time when the Israelites were dying from the bites of poisonous snakes (Numbers 21:5-9). To remedy the situation, God instructed Moses to make a bronze serpent and place it on a pole so that anyone who was bitten would be healed by merely looking at the serpent on the pole. In like manner, Jesus would also be lifted up (on the cross), so that whoever believes in Him can have eternal life.

The story of the serpent on the pole is a *living parable;* a story that *pairs well* with what Jesus was going to do on the cross.

2nd Corinthians 5:21 For he hath made him to be sin for us, who knew no sin; that we might be made the righteousness of God in him.

It is normal for God to write deeper meaning into the stories and lives of His people. We find it over and over again throughout His written Word. As we shall see, *Ruth* is no exception. In fact, it is likely one of the most powerful *living parables* in the Bible.

The Name of God

Whatever happened to the name of God as found in the Old
Testament is a rather interesting, if not sad, curiosity. We read
the narratives and find that His personal name was used often,
and by people of all walks of life. They knew God's name and
spoke it. But in many of our Bibles, rather than reading His actual
name as it was used, the English translations have the word *LORD*
in all capital letters where the actual Hebrew text has the
personal name for God. The people of Israel used to know that
name. Now no one knows it, even though it is written in Hebrew
throughout the Old Testament for all to see.

We call it the *Tetragrammaton,* which consists of four Hebrew
letters with no vowels (Hebrew does not have vowels in its
alphabet). These letters have been translated to our English
equivalents, JHVH and YHWH. The problem is that without
vowels, the correct pronunciation of the Name has been lost. To
remedy this, vowels have been placed between the consonants,
and we are given two choices by the scholars: Jehovah (JHVH)
and Yahweh (YHWH). Yet neither can claim a title of absolute
correctness because we simply do not know how His name was
pronounced in ancient Israel.

Also, the pronunciation of *Ys* and *Js* and *Ws* and *Vs* can vary, even
in within the same spoken language. Today, Yahweh has become
the more popular name for God, but most English Bibles simply
use the four letters that spell LORD, in order to avoid confusion.
Everyone knows who the LORD is.

For this work, wherever the name of God becomes a special topic of our attention, I have chosen to use *Yahweh;* not because I think it is the better of the two choices we are given. It is merely the more popular of the two in today's society.

GOEL

גָּאַל

gâ'al *gaw-al'*

A primitive root, to *redeem* (according to the
Oriental law of kinship), i.e. to *be the next of kin*
(and as such to *buy back* a relative's property, *marry
his widow, etc.*): -   X in any wise, X at all, avenger,
deliver, (do, perform the part of near, next) kinsfolk
(-man), purchase, ransom, redeem (-er), revenger.

-   *Strong's Hebrew Dictionary*

———————

GOEL - The Kinsman-Redeemer

In the book of Ruth, the entire story is hinged on the *goel*. The *goel* (properly pronounced, gaw-al') was a Hebrew designation for the man who was responsible for his next of kin, in the event of misfortune or tragedy. We know from the Scriptures that his responsibility was at least fourfold.

The *goel* could redeem property (Leviticus 25:25). If his brother became poor and was forced to sell his property, the *goel*, if able, could buy it back and restore it to his brother. He could also redeem a brother from slavery (Leviticus 25:47-49). The *goel* was also the *avenger of blood*. If a member of the family was murdered, it was the duty of the *goel* to slay the murderer (Deut. 19:11-12). Finally, the *goel* was able to restore the name of the dead among his people. If a brother, or close relative died and left a widow with no child, the *goel* was expected to marry her, and her firstborn son would continue the name of the brother who died, that his name not be cut off from Israel (Deut. 25:5-6).

The Hebrew Scriptures call this man the *goel*. We call him the kinsman-redeemer.

Introduction to the Story

Aside from the theological undertones (those living parables) that run throughout the narrative, *Ruth* contains everything one might expect to find in a well written story of tragedy, love, hope, and restoration. Beginning with a famine, it spirals downward into hopelessness and despair with the deaths of Elimelech and his two sons, only to hang onto a thread of mere existence as the widow Ruth works the fields to provide food for herself and Naomi, her widowed mother-in-law.

Enter Boaz, and the story begins to move from despair toward hope. Boaz remains an obscure hero until the end of the second chapter. Ruth does not know the man other than his name and that he owns the field where she worked, and that he treated her very well.

The story reaches its first climax when Naomi learns that it is Boaz who owns the land, and was kind toward Ruth. This is at once both a surprise and a source of hope and restored joy for Naomi. It is also a surprise to the first time reader (or listener) of the Hebrew text; for the revelation of Boaz to Naomi becomes the revelation of the *goel* to everyone (this is the first appearance of *goel* in the story). Boaz is the *goel,* the kinsman-redeemer of Naomi's dead husband.

This sets in motion some planning and strategy, some risk taking and another climactic surprise, with a twist and secrecy leading to a glorious ending; which is also a new beginning. Best of all, it is real history, with God in control.

Chapter 1

The Famine

Man does not live by bread alone, but man lives by every word that comes from the mouth of the LORD.

Deuteronomy 8:3 (ESV)

Whenever the LORD creates a disturbance to restore His people to Himself, families and individuals are affected in various ways, and react accordingly. It is here that we find the hand of God at work in individual lives. The book of Ruth recounts one such experience.

Ruth 1:1 Now it came to pass in the days when the judges ruled, that there was a famine in the land. And a certain man of Bethlehemjudah went to sojourn in the country of Moab, he, and his wife, and his two sons. 1:2 And the name of the man was Elimelech, and the name of his wife Naomi, and the name of his two sons Mahlon and Chilion, Ephrathites of Bethlehemjudah. And they came into the country of Moab, and continued there.

Ezekiel 14:21 tells us that *famine* is one God's four severe judgments. Ruth opens with a famine during the *days when the judges ruled*. Those were turbulent times, as the children of Israel did evil in the sight of the LORD, and repeatedly turned from God to serve the gods of the people in the land (Judges 2:11-12; 3:7, 12; 4:1; 6:1; 10:6; 13:1). The physical *famine* here in Ruth may well have resulted from a spiritual famine, as the people continually turned from their true Source of life.

God works in the small things. Our tendency is to look for Him in greatness. While the history of His activity shows some occasion for this, more often He is at work where no one is looking, and where you would never expect.

And greatness is surprisingly found in the small things. In *Ruth*, we find God at work in a famine, which prodded a man named Elimelech to leave his home and move his family to Moab.

And the Woman was Left

For unto you it is given in the behalf of Christ, not only to believe on him, but also to suffer for his sake

Philippians 1:29

Genesis 2:24 Therefore shall a man leave his father and his mother, and shall cleave unto his wife: and they shall be one flesh.

Ruth 1:3 And Elimelech Naomi's husband died; and she was left, and her two sons.
1:4 And they took them wives of the women of Moab; the name of the one was Orpah, and the name of the other Ruth: and they dwelled there about ten years.
1:5 And Mahlon and Chilion died also both of them; and the woman was left of her two sons and her husband.

This story opens in tragedy. And though this is a very ancient story, we would do well to understand it as something that really happened to real people in real time. We are introduced by name to Elimelech and his two sons. All three died untimely deaths, leaving behind their wives, who would obviously have been traumatized. Naomi, Elimelech's wife, was hardest hit, losing her husband and both her sons. When Naomi's husband died, her own flesh died. When her two sons died, she lost her own flesh and blood. Naomi's wound was deep; and her pain, real.

Like severed nerves in physical trauma, bereavement brings with it a kind of numbness, mingled with an erratic and agonizing emotional pain. Accustomed to having a loved one with us all the time, we may feel that he or she is still *here*. The general feeling is that they are in the next room, or out somewhere and we expect to see them again as usual.

But that same moment brings with it the grim reminder. It's like losing an arm. You are so used to it being there that you expect to use it, but it's not there anymore. You have lost part of yourself.

When the pain begins, it is unbearable. For weeks, months, sometimes for years, overwhelming grief floods the soul sporadically, and wailing is normal. Make no mistake. Naomi was absolutely devastated. But even so, God was in control; and He still is. And yes, I have been down that road.

Romans 8:18 For I reckon that the sufferings of this present time are not worthy to be compared with the glory which shall be revealed in us.

Naomi's valley was the beginning of her upward ascent on a mountain of glory. This we know. We have the rest of her story. And we can have the same confidence as our stories continue, with God in control.

Romans 15:4 For whatever things were written before were written for our instruction, that through patience and encouragement of the Scriptures we might have hope. (LITV)

The War

And the dragon was wroth with the woman

Revelation 12:17

Genesis 3:15 And I will put enmity between thee and the woman, and between thy seed and her seed; it shall bruise thy head, and thou shalt bruise his heel.

Ruth, in its proper biblical context, takes its place as one theater in a war that God had declared ages before.

Genesis 3:13 And the LORD God said unto the woman, What is this that thou hast done? And the woman said, The serpent beguiled me, and I did eat.
3:14 And the LORD God said unto the serpent, Because thou hast done this, thou art cursed above all cattle, and above every beast of the field; upon thy belly shalt thou go, and dust shalt thou eat all the days of thy life:
3:15 And I will put enmity between thee and the woman, and between thy seed and her seed; it shall bruise thy head, and thou shalt bruise his heel.

Immediately after the temptation and fall of Adam and Eve, God declared war. He named the participants: the serpent (also called Satan, Rev. 12:9) and the woman. This war would span the generations, between the serpent's seed and the seed (descendants) of the woman (*thy seed and her seed*). In the end, the seed of the woman would defeat the serpent (*bruise thy head*), but not without being hurt (the serpent would *bruise his heal*).

From that time forward, the war was on. In hindsight, we can see the devastation: of Cain murdering Abel (Gen. 4:8); of the violence that led to the Great Flood (Gen. 6:13); of Pharaoh's attempt to kill all male Hebrew babies (Ex. 1:16); of King Herod's slaughter of Bethlehem's children (Mat. 2:16). Satan and his seed left no stone unturned in relentless pursuit to stop the promised seed; the seed of the woman.

Within this line of progression in this battle of the ages, *Ruth* opens with a victory for the devil: three dead, and no seed. But this story is not over; and if you are reading this, neither is yours.

The Living Parable

When it seems things are falling apart, they may really be falling
into place.

- *Source unknown*

John 12:24 Most assuredly, I say to you, unless a grain of wheat falls into the ground and dies, it remains alone; but if it dies, it produces much grain. (NKJV)

The Word of God is multifaceted. It is multi-dimensional. It is simple, yet unfathomable. But if in searching the Scriptures, we find Jesus, we have all we need.

In Hebrew, the name, Elimelech, means *God is King*. Mahlon means *Weakness*, or *Sickly*. Chilion means *Pining*. The nation of Moab was named for its founder, who was the son of Abraham's nephew Lot and Lot's firstborn daughter (Genesis 19:36-37). She named him Moab, which means, *Of His Father*. There is a reason we are given all of these names here at the start of the book of Ruth.

Proverbs 25:2 It is the glory of God to conceal a thing: but the honor of kings is to search out a matter.

The significance of the names cannot go without mention. They were planted within the context of this historical narrative and remained there without much notice for centuries; until Jesus came. Jesus is the game changer. Like the sun and the rain, He brings light and life in the most unexpected places. *"Search the Scriptures,"* He tells us. *"They testify of Me"* (John 5:39). In *Ruth,* the names are essential in this living parable of Jesus Christ.

The town of *Bethlehemjudah* is a short way of saying *the town of Bethlehem in the land of Judah.* Bethlehem means *House of Bread.* Judah means *Praise*. The simple story is that Elimelech left Bethlehemjudah to dwell in the land of Moab, where he and his two sons died.

The living parable says this: *God is King* left the *House of Bread* in the land of *Praise* to dwell in a foreign land called *Of His Father*. *God is King* died there with his two sons, *Weakness* and *Pining*.

The reality is Jesus Christ. He is *God* incarnate and *King* of kings. He left His *House* (He Himself is the *Bread:* the Bread of life – John 6:48). He left His *Land,* the habitation of eternal *Praise*. He came into this world as into a foreign land, and it was *Of His Father*.

As with Elimelech, two other deaths were linked with His. He was numbered with the transgressors (Isaiah 53:12; Mark 15:28). The two men crucified on either side of Him died as a result of their own poor choices in life. We might easily label them *Weakness* and *Pining*. One of them would go with Jesus into Paradise (Luke 23:43). And one of Elimelech's sons was married to Ruth. There *is* hope beyond the grave.

The Hearing Ear

Like cold water to a thirsty soul, so is good news from a far country.

Proverbs 25:25 (ESV)

To guard from the danger of outlaws and wild beasts, people traveled by caravan in ancient times. And it is not unlikely that over the years, one would see familiar faces time and again as travelers passed through the region. They might bring with them food and merchandise from the places they had been. They might also have news from faraway.

Ruth 1:6 Then she arose with her daughters in law, that she might return from the country of Moab: for she had heard in the country of Moab how that the LORD had visited his people in giving them bread.
1:7 Wherefore she went forth out of the place where she was, and her two daughters in law with her; and they went on the way to return unto the land of Judah.

There was word that God had visited His people back in Judah *in giving them bread*. Remember that Judah means *praise.* This was good news from the land of praise. Naomi *heard* it, and believed what she heard. That's called faith. Upon hearing this word about what God had done, she left her *place* in Moab to *return unto the land of Judah.* This is faith in action.

Romans 10:17 So then faith cometh by hearing, and hearing by the word of God.

As it was with Naomi, there is good news from the *Land of Praise* for us today; because 2,000 years ago, the LORD visited His people, and gave *us* Bread. Jesus is the *Bread of God* (John 6:33).

The Name of God

Though he slay me, yet will I trust in him

Job13:15

It is likely that Naomi and her two daughters-in-law initially set out together to join a caravan traveling toward Judah. They are probably at the caravan at this point, where Naomi's journey would begin.

Ruth 1:8 And Naomi said unto her two daughters in law, Go, return each to her mother's house: the LORD deal kindly with you, as ye have dealt with the dead, and with me.
1:9 The LORD grant you that ye may find rest, each of you in the house of her husband. Then she kissed them; and they lifted up their voice, and wept.

We might compare this scene to accompanying a loved one to a train station or airport to see them off. In saying good-bye, Naomi began to invoke blessings from the *LORD* on their behalf. And from this we get a glimpse of Naomi's faith.

Recall that the times of the judges were known for Israel's idolatry. The people of Israel turned away from the LORD to worship other gods. But here we learn that Naomi, even in her darkest hour, honored God. And she said His name; for the word, *LORD*, more correctly translated, is *Yahweh*. It is the personal name for God.

Naomi named *Yahweh* as the Source for kindness and rest toward her daughters-in-law. The Moabites worshiped a "god" called Chemosh. But Naomi glorified Yahweh as God. Her world had fallen apart, but Naomi's faith in God remained unshaken.

dealt with the dead (v. 8)

Don't miss this. Naomi said that her daughters-in-law had kindly *dealt with the dead*. She did not say that they were kind to her sons while they lived, although this is likely what she meant. The text is specific, and says that they kindly *dealt with the dead.* The inspired Word has it preserved that way for a reason. This is a story of hope, and not merely hope for the living. We will see this again.

The Kiss

For whosoever will save his life shall lose it

Luke 9:24

Ruth 1:10 And they said unto her, Surely we will return with thee unto thy people.

1:11 And Naomi said, Turn again, my daughters: why will ye go with me? Are there yet any more sons in my womb, that they may be your husbands?

1:12 Turn again, my daughters, go your way; for I am too old to have an husband. If I should say, I have hope, if I should have an husband also to night, and should also bear sons; 1:13 Would ye tarry for them till they were grown? would ye stay for them from having husbands? nay, my daughters; for it grieveth me much for your sakes that the hand of the LORD is gone out against me.

1:14 And they lifted up their voice, and wept again: and Orpah kissed her mother in law; but Ruth clave unto her.

These verses reveal some of the psychological instability that often accompanies ongoing emotional trauma. Naomi's husband died. Naomi's sons died. Naomi's obvious conclusion was that *the hand of the LORD* was against her. It appears that in her thinking, *she* was the source of suffering for both her daughters-in-law as well as herself. But we know differently. We have the whole story. There are other things at work which Naomi knows nothing about. And blessings emerge from the lowest of places.

As hopeless as things seem at this point in Naomi's life, better things are coming. And these things were written for us so that we might be encouraged, particularly in difficult times.

why will ye go with me? ...

... for it grieveth me much for your sakes that the hand of the LORD is gone out against me. (vv. 11, 13)

All that falls between those two statements comprise Naomi's rationale to convince them to go home. She asks leading questions to which the obvious answers are *no*. Does she have other sons for them to marry? She's too old for a husband, and even if she had one, would they wait and refrain from marrying until her children were grown? And she's asking these things with tears running down her cheeks. She really believed that it would be better for them to return to their homes where they might have hope for another husband. She wanted what was best for them.

and Orpah kissed her mother in law; (v. 14)

Initially, both girls would have accompanied Naomi back to her land, but Naomi's words convinced Orpah to stay. This was a kiss good-bye. Orpah did the right thing, as far as she knew. It made sense. It was practical. It was Naomi's desire for her. Most people would have done the same thing. But this is where Orpah's story ends, and Ruth's begins.

The Living Sacrifice

... but whosoever will lose his life for my sake

Luke 9:24

Ruth 1:14 And they lifted up their voice, and wept again: and Orpah kissed her mother in law; but Ruth clave unto her.

1:15 And she said, Behold, thy sister in law is gone back unto her people, and unto her gods: return thou after thy sister in law.

1:16 And Ruth said, Intreat me not to leave thee, or to return from following after thee: for whither thou goest, I will go; and where thou lodgest, I will lodge: thy people shall be my people, and thy God my God:

1:17 Where thou diest, will I die, and there will I be buried: the LORD do so to me, and more also, if ought but death part thee and me.

1:18 When she saw that she was stedfastly minded to go with her, then she left speaking unto her.

The beauty of this story, from which we can all learn, is the beauty of sacrifice. Ruth sacrificed everything she knew to be with this woman, Naomi. Her love for her mother-in-law poured deep. She was told to leave. She was told that there was nothing for her; nothing to gain, as far as Ruth was concerned. But Ruth was more concerned about Naomi than her own well-being. Naomi insisted that she go back with her sister-in-law. In so many words, Ruth replied, *I will never leave you nor forsake you.*

The Helper

... but Ruth clave unto her.

Ruth 1:14

Ephesians 5:31 For this cause shall a man leave his father and mother, and shall be joined unto his wife, and they two shall be one flesh.
5:32 This is a great mystery: but I speak concerning Christ and the church.

Naomi means, *My Delight*. She is the bride of the one who died, whose name means, *God is King*. She is the woman who was left. And we know that Jesus also left His bride, which is His church; His delight. But He did not leave her alone. He sent His Spirit.

John 16:7 Nevertheless I tell you the truth; It is expedient for you that I go away: for if I go not away, the Comforter will not come unto you; but if I depart, I will send him unto you.

The word, *Comforter,* is a translation of the original Greek word, *parakletos.* It means *one who is called to one's side. Companion* is another translation of the same word. Jesus sent His Spirit to be our *Companion* to comfort us during our pilgrimage here on earth. And so it was with Naomi. For while Naomi groaned how the Almighty had afflicted her, there was one who *clave unto her,* who shared in her suffering, who would never leave nor forsake her. The name, Ruth, means *Companion*.

Call Me Mara

... the LORD hath testified against me

Ruth 1:21

Ruth 1:19 So they two went until they came to Bethlehem. And it came to pass, when they were come to Bethlehem, that all the city was moved about them, and they said, Is this Naomi?
1:20 And she said unto them, Call me not Naomi, call me Mara: for the Almighty hath dealt very bitterly with me.
1:21 I went out full, and the LORD hath brought me home again empty: why then call ye me Naomi, seeing the LORD hath testified against me, and the Almighty hath afflicted me?

What a joy to see Naomi again! Or was it? *Call me Mara*, she said. *Mara* means *Bitterness*. Quite understandably, Naomi was bitter. She lost her husband. She lost both her sons. She was too old to marry, and her only companion, her daughter-in-law, was not of her people. Ruth was a Moabite, forbidden to enter into the congregation of the LORD (Deut. 23:3). It seemed the only thing left for Naomi to do was to live out the rest of her life and die a bereaved widow, with no hope of seeing any posterity.

Did you ever know someone going through the fiery trial? It's not uncommon for people to be angry with God. Nor is it uncommon for people to curse God. None of that is beyond God's power to forgive. He knows we are weak. Job is the exception, not the rule. Most people aren't Job, and God knows that. Naomi didn't curse God, but she certainly laid the cause for her suffering at His doorstep; and rightly so, for even Satan cannot touch God's people without His consent (Job 1:11-12; 2:3-6; Luke 22:31-32).

God has the bottom line signature. And He is always on our side working things for our good, to bring us into His likeness. And that takes some suffering on our part.

Whatever suffering you experience, whether from a direct consequence of sin, or a trial that has come into your life, or even outright persecution, the bottom line is that God is in charge, working all things for good; even when it doesn't seem like it. And God is at work here, at the bottom of the Valley of Naomi.

Ruth 1:22 So Naomi returned, and Ruth the Moabitess, her daughter in law, with her, which returned out of the country of Moab: and they came to Bethlehem in the beginning of barley harvest.

The bottom of the valley is the beginning of the mountain. This chapter opened with a famine in the first verse, and went downhill from there. We are now at the bottom of that hill, and at the end of the chapter, where the last word is *harvest*. Things are looking up.

Chapter 2

And His Name was Boaz

Matthew 5:4 *Blessed are they that mourn: for they shall be comforted.*

- Jesus Christ

The first chapter ended with Naomi in misery. God had dealt bitterly with her; or so it seemed. But here at the beginning of Chapter 2, we who sit on the sidelines, we the audience, get a piece of narration that Naomi knows nothing about.

Ruth 2:1 And Naomi had a kinsman of her husband's, a mighty man of wealth, of the family of Elimelech; and his name was Boaz.

Suddenly we are introduced to a man named Boaz, who is a *kinsman* of Elimelech; *a mighty man of wealth*. There is a reason for telling us this. This man Boaz is going to be a major player. *Boaz* is an interesting name. Scholars are uncertain of its origin, but the consensus is that it signifies *swiftness* and *strength*. The fact that he is a *kinsman* is noteworthy; but we are not told, not yet, how significant this Boaz is going to be.

Boaz is a sort of like Jesus this way. For many of us, we hear about Jesus, and he seems like some obscure but great man of history. We have no idea how great He really is. But the closer we get to Him, the more we learn of Him, the greater He becomes. And when our eyes are opened so that we truly see Him, our lives are transformed. Naomi is in for a surprise. This Boaz is going to be an eye-opener.

So maybe things aren't as bad as Naomi's misery makes them out to be. That doesn't change the tragedy she's had to endure. That doesn't stop the pain. But God is at work, and we are introduced to Boaz. Naomi does not know it, but she is about to be comforted.

God's Provision

When thou cuttest down thine harvest in thy field, and hast forgot a sheaf ....

Deuteronomy 24:19

Ruth and Naomi had arrived in Bethlehem. Both are widows. Ruth is a widow and a stranger. And here we learn one of the ways of God; for God had commanded the Israelites to care for their widows and orphans, and also the stranger.

Leviticus 23:22 And when you reap the harvest of your land, you shall not completely reap the corners of your field when you reap, neither shall you gather any gleaning of your harvest: you shall leave them unto the poor, and to the stranger: I am the LORD your God. (KJV 2000)

God ensured that provision was made for the poor, but the poor still had to work for it. Unlike today's society, there were no free handouts in God's economy. The poor were allowed to glean the fields after the reapers and take up what was left behind. This is a lesson and an example for every society in providing for their poor.

Deuteronomy 24:19 When thou cuttest down thine harvest in thy field, and hast forgot a sheaf in the field, thou shalt not go again to fetch it: it shall be for the stranger, for the fatherless, and for the widow: that the LORD thy God may bless thee in all the work of thine hands.

Do you ever wonder why you forget some things? And later, maybe it turns out to be a good thing you forgot. God knows how to take care of those who depend on Him, and sometimes there are reasons for our forgetfulness.

Gleaning after the Reapers

It is better to go to the house of mourning, than to go to the house of feasting

Ecclesiastes 7:2

Ruth 2:2 And Ruth the Moabitess said unto Naomi, Let me now go to the field, and glean ears of grain after him in whose sight I shall find grace. And she said unto her, Go, my daughter.

Ruth is doing what she can to care for Naomi. She is going to work in order to provide for their needs. She will go behind the reapers and glean what is left behind.

Ruth 2:3 And she went, and came, and gleaned in the field after the reapers: and her hap was to light on a part of the field belonging unto Boaz, who was of the kindred of Elimelech

What does it mean to glean *after the reapers*? There is more to this picture than meets the eye. Sometimes when loved ones pass away, we say that the angels came and took them away. Jesus said this about a man who died; a poor beggar named Lazarus (Luke 16:20-22).

Luke 16:22 And it came to pass, that the beggar died, and was carried by the angels into Abraham's bosom:

When the angels come and carry away our loved ones, it is devastating to those of us who are left behind, and we need time; time to just sit; to pray; to wail; to be angry; to grieve deeply; and to recover. It is good to have someone to come and help pick up the pieces. Naomi's wound is deep. She is probably numb. Ruth is doing what she can to hold things together in spite of her own loss. She is gleaning the fields after the reapers in more ways than one.

Matthew 13:39 … and the reapers are the angels.

It was Ruth's *hap* to come upon that *part of the field belonging to Boaz.* In gleaning after the reapers, she entered the land of him whose name means *Strength.* It was her *hap,* and it followed what she did.

Strength Came from Bethlehem

For when we were yet without strength

Romans 5:6

Ruth 2:4 And, behold, Boaz came from Bethlehem, and said unto the reapers, The LORD be with you. And they answered him, The LORD bless thee.

Does anyone else see Christ and the angels here? If you know the story, then you know Boaz will be the redeemer. What other Redeemer came from Bethlehem? Who are the reapers? The picture has always been there. It was there before Jesus came. But we couldn't see it until after He came.

Boaz (or *Strength*), came from Bethlehem. *Strength* came from Bethlehem. In the greater scheme of things, this would be the understatement of eternity. We could retell the story of Ruth and Naomi and their loss. We could tell of their hopeless condition. But *Strength* came from Bethlehem. Boaz is the hinge on which this whole story takes a turn, from despair to hope. Boaz is sort of like Jesus this way, for Christ is the hinge on which all human history is balanced. Time itself is numbered around His birth. And without Jesus, there is no hope.

God with Us

And there were in the same country shepherds
abiding in the field

Luke 2:8

Ruth 2:4 And, behold, Boaz came from Bethlehem, and said unto the reapers, The LORD be with you.

Did you hear what Boaz said? In greeting the reapers, he also made what we might call a *prophetic* statement. He said, "*The LORD be with you.*" While this may appear to be a common form of greeting, there are only two verses in all of Scripture where this phrase stands alone in a single sentence. The first is here. The other is in the New Testament, in 2nd Thessalonians 3:16. Here, it is a greeting. There, it is a farewell. Both address the people of God. But here, there is an additional element. These people were *Bethlehemites*.

Boaz said, "**The LORD be with you.**" And it happened. And it happened in *Bethlehem*.

Matthew 1:22 Now all this was done, that it might be fulfilled which was spoken of the Lord by the prophet, saying,
1:23 Behold, a virgin shall be with child, and shall bring forth a son, and they shall call his name Emmanuel, which being interpreted is, God with us.

Boaz made the statement to Bethlehemites working in the fields, harvesting grain used to make bread. About a thousand years later, the fulfillment of these words will also be announced; to Bethlehemites working in the fields. But they won't be harvesting. They will be watching over sheep. For Jesus, who is the *Bread of Life*, is also the *Lamb of God*.

And they answered him, The LORD bless thee. Ruth 2:4

These people of Bethlehem honored God in the way they greeted Boaz. A ray of God's kingdom shone through Boaz and these people of Bethlehem. Should it not shine through us as well?

Matthew 5:16 Let your light so shine before men

Whose damsel is this?

And when the king came in to see the guests,
he saw there a man

Matthew 22:11

Ruth 2:5 Then said Boaz unto his servant that was set over the reapers, Whose damsel is this?

There is a new face among the reapers. Boaz wants to know who she is. Jesus told a parable similar to what we have in this scene. It is about a king who found a stranger among his guests at a wedding feast.

Matthew 22:11 And when the king came in to see the guests, he saw there a man which had not on a wedding garment:
22:12 And he saith unto him, Friend, how camest thou in hither not having a wedding garment? And he was speechless.

The outcome for this man with no wedding garment was not good. So what is this wedding garment, and why is it necessary? Keep in mind that the church of Christ is also the bride of Christ, and every bride has her wedding garment.

Revelation 19:7 Let us be glad and rejoice, and give honor to Him: for the marriage of the Lamb is come, and his wife has made herself ready.
19:8 And to her was granted that she should be arrayed in fine linen, clean and white: for the fine linen is the righteous acts of saints.

The wedding garment symbolizes the righteous acts, or the good things the believer in Christ has done. Good works that glorify God are the natural outcome of one who has been born of God.

Ephesians 2:10 For we are his workmanship, created in Christ Jesus unto good works, which God hath before ordained that we should walk in them.

Note that we do not do good works to obtain God's favor so that He might save us. Rather, it is because we are *His workmanship, created in Christ Jesus unto good works*, that we should produce good works. If God is at work on the inside of us by His Spirit, then the fruit of the Spirit will be revealed in our day to day activities; our works. We *should walk in them.* In other words, we should be known by our good works as if we wore them like a garment.

The man at the wedding did not have a wedding garment. We might say that he had no *good works*. He lacked the identifying *garment* necessary for acceptance before the king. In contrast, we have Ruth, who has put her own life aside to care for someone else, and now the master is asking about her. Do you suppose Ruth is wearing the right *garment*?

Whose damsel is this? (2:5)

We cannot leave this passage without a word on Boaz and his first impression of Ruth. *Whose damsel is this?* Those were the first words out of his mouth after greeting the workers. He said nothing of how the work was progressing, or if they were having any problems. No, but his eyes were fixed on the new girl. Ruth must have been a very attractive young lady; at least to Boaz. Her presence commanded his attention. This too may be a living parable.

Meeting Ruth

… that they may see your good works

Matthew 5:16

Ruth 2:6 And the servant that was set over the reapers answered and said, It is the Moabitish damsel that came back with Naomi out of the country of Moab: 2:7 And she said, I pray you, let me glean and gather after the reapers among the sheaves: so she came, and hath continued even from the morning until now, that she tarried a little in the house.

The head reaper commends Ruth. He tells Boaz who she is, the *Moabitish damsel that came back with Naomi.* Everyone had already heard of her. Ruth's reputation preceded her. No further description was necessary. He then tells Boaz why she is there, and how she had worked up to the time he arrived as they were taking a break at the house. Ruth's selfless devotion toward Naomi, and her hard work on that day marked her as one worthy of praise. In other words, Ruth wore the right *garment*. If Boaz was attracted to this girl's physical appearance, how much more now, having learned who she is?

And this living parable continues. Will you be with the reapers at the harvest? Will you be found among the angels in the mansion of Him whose name is *Strength*? Are you wearing the right *garment*?

Hearest Thou Not?

So then faith cometh by hearing

Romans 10:17

Ruth 2:8 Then said Boaz unto Ruth, Hearest thou not, my daughter? Go not to glean in another field, neither go from hence, but abide here fast by my maidens: 2:9 Let thine eyes be on the field that they do reap, and go thou after them: have I not charged the young men that they shall not touch thee? and when thou art athirst, go unto the vessels, and drink of that which the young men have drawn.

Boaz does not want to lose this one! He told her not to glean any place else! In the presence of everyone, Boaz promoted Ruth from gathering whatever was left, to work alongside his own maidens. And the young men heard his words. They were not to touch her. And if she got thirsty, they were to draw water for her.

God looks after those who draw near to Him. He knows those who glean the fields after the reapers. He asks if we hear Him. *Hearest thou not?* Faith comes by hearing, and hearing by the word of God (Romans 10:17). And if we hear Him, will we do what He tells us, and *abide*? He directs our eyes to His *field*, and calls us to the harvest. He has charged his reapers not to harm us. In fact, they will serve us, for they are ministers to the heirs of salvation.

Hebrews 1:13 But to which of the angels said he at any time, Sit on my right hand, until I make thine enemies thy footstool? 1:14 Are they not all ministering spirits, sent forth to minister for them who shall be heirs of salvation?

She Fell Down

… a Moabite shall not enter into the assembly of the LORD

Deuteronomy 23:3

Ruth 2:10 Then she fell on her face, and bowed herself to the ground, and said unto him, Why have I found grace in thine eyes, that thou shouldest take knowledge of me, seeing I am a stranger?

She fell down and bowed before Boaz. Ruth is obviously overwhelmed, taken by surprise. She can only ask why this man would bestow such unexpected kindness on her behalf. She is not of his people. She is a stranger in his land. Less than a stranger, she is a Moabite, marked by the LORD.

Deuteronomy 23:3 An Ammonite or a Moabite shall not enter into the assembly of the LORD; even to the tenth generation shall none belonging to them enter into the assembly of the LORD for ever 23:4 because they met you not with bread and with water in the way, when ye came forth out of Egypt; and because they hired against thee Balaam the son of Beor from Pethor of Mesopotamia, to curse thee.

When we understand the low social status of a Moabite in Israel, it is no wonder that Ruth would be surprised and overwhelmed. But she doesn't know Boaz. Not yet.

Is Ruth not a picture of us? Like Ruth, we too are outsiders. Sin has separated us from God, and we have no standing in His presence. But like Ruth, we have our Boaz. His name is Jesus. Do you know Him?

The scene painted in this passage is no coincidence. This is a graphic picture of the believer in Jesus Christ in that great and final Day. When all is said and done, and we, like Ruth, find ourselves among the reapers before the Master, recipients of His grace and counted worthy to abide safely in His presence, we too will fall down.

The Broken Wall

(A story behind the story)

There once was a young man and a young woman who were separated by a great wall. The name of the man was Salmon, and the woman's name was Rahab. Salmon was on the outside of the wall, and Rahab was on the inside of it. Salmon was a soldier of Israel, a mighty man of valor. Rahab was a Canaanite, a harlot of Jericho; and the wall was the wall of Jericho.

We learn in the book of *Joshua* that the wall of Jericho fell at the voice of trumpets, and by the shouts of the armies of Israel (Joshua 6:20). The city of Jericho was destroyed, but Rahab and her family was saved from the destruction; for she had previously saved two Israelite spies from being captured.

With Jericho destroyed, Rahab now belonged with Israel. But she had a problem. Rahab was a known harlot by occupation; a sinful woman. She was also a Canaanite, an outsider among the Israelites. Although she had previously saved the two Israelite spies (Joshua 2), it did not change her past or her status. But Salmon loved Rahab, and she became his bride. Interestingly, the name Salmon means *Garment*. Rahab was covered.

Salmon is sort of like Christ this way, and we are like Rahab. We all have a past, and are sinners by nature, separated from God. But like Rahab, we too have a bridegroom. His name is Jesus, and He covers us with His *garment*, which is the righteousness of God.

Romans 3:22 Even the righteousness of God which is by faith of Jesus Christ unto all and upon all them that believe: for there is no difference:

But before the marriage, before the *Garment*, the wall of Jericho had to come down. This, too, is a living parable, a foreshadowing of Jesus Christ.

Ephesians 2:13 But now in Christ Jesus ye who sometimes were far off are made near by the blood of Christ.
2:14 For he is our peace, who hath made both one, and hath broken down the middle wall of partition between us;

And so the wall was broken down, and Salmon married Rahab. They became one; and gave birth to a son, and called his name, *Boaz*.

Matthew 1:5 and to Salmon was born Boaz by Rahab (NAS 1977)

Both Israelite and Canaanite, Boaz could identify with an outsider like Ruth. And Jesus Christ, both God and Man, has identified with us.

John 1:1 In the beginning was the Word, and the Word was with God, and the Word was God.

John 1:14 And the Word became flesh and dwelt among us (ESV)

After the Death

For ye are dead, and your life is hid with Christ in God.

Colossians 3:3

Ruth 2:11 And Boaz answered and said unto her, It hath fully been shewed me, all that thou hast done unto thy mother in law since the death of thine husband: and how thou hast left thy father and thy mother, and the land of thy nativity, and art come unto a people which thou knewest not heretofore.
2:12 The LORD recompense thy work, and a full reward be given thee of the LORD God of Israel, under whose wings thou art come to trust.

Recall that it was after the death of Naomi's husband (her own flesh by marriage) that her woeful pilgrimage began, unto the land of *Praise* (Judah). And here, Ruth is *praised* and blessed by the master of the harvest in that very land. And as it was with Naomi and her journey, everything that Ruth did for which Boaz commended her she did *after the death* of her own flesh (by marriage). We know nothing of Ruth until after this death. Likewise, our pilgrimage and works begin after *our* death; our death with Christ, our Bridegroom.

Romans 6:4 therefore we are buried with him by baptism into death: that like as Christ was raised up from the dead by the glory of the Father, even so we also should walk in newness of life.

His Name's Sake

Matthew 19:29 And every one that hath forsaken houses, or brethren, or sisters, or father, or mother, or wife, or children, or lands, for my name's sake …

When Boaz recognized Ruth's kindness toward Naomi, he also mentioned something else she did.

...and how thou hast left thy father and thy mother, and the land of thy nativity, and art come unto a people which thou knewest not heretofore. (2:11)

And then he adds:

Ruth 2:12 May Yahweh reward your work and may a full reward be given to you from Yahweh, the God of Israel, under whose wings you came to take refuge." (LEB)

Verse twelve is taken from the *Lexham English Bible*. The inspired Scripture has Boaz calling on the personal name of God, and we do not want to miss that; not here. When Ruth left her father and mother, and the land of her nativity, she also left Chemosh, Moab's god. *Yahweh* had become the name of Ruth's God.

Not many people forsake *everything* as Ruth did. Like her sister Orpah, Ruth could have sought a second chance for a new husband and a better life. That would have been normal, for this is the way of the world. What Ruth did was not normal.

It was life-changing.

Comforted

This is my comfort in my affliction, for Your word has given me life.

Psalm 119:50 (NKJV)

Ruth 2:13 Then she said, "I have found favor in your sight, my lord, for you have comforted me and indeed have spoken kindly to your maidservant, though I am not like one of your maidservants." (NASB)

This may be the first time Ruth experienced a measure of comfort since her husband died. Up to this point, she had been tending to the needs of Naomi. While we have Naomi's words that reveal her pain through her grieving, we have no idea what Ruth was going through. It may be that helping Naomi also helped Ruth to focus on something other than her own pain. Sometimes it becomes necessary to change focus. Helping Naomi led Ruth to the fields of Boaz, where in setting her own life aside for someone else, she received comfort.

Matthew 10:39 … and he that loseth his life for my sake shall find it.

Ruth is beginning to find her life.

The Master's Table

Thou preparest a table before me

Psalm 23:5

Luke 22:27 For who is the greater, one who reclines at table or one who serves? Is it not the one who reclines at table? But I am among you as the one who serves.

Ruth 2:14 And at mealtime Boaz said to her, "Come here and eat some bread and dip your morsel in the wine." So she sat beside the reapers, and he passed to her roasted grain. And she ate until she was satisfied, and she had some left over. (ESV)

Ruth is again elevated by the master of the harvest, as he invited her to his table to sit among his chosen ones. And he personally served her. She was satisfied with more than enough. She has leftovers, and she will save them for someone special. We might say that her cup was running over.

Handfuls on Purpose

For he will command his angels concerning you

Psalm 91:11 (ESV)

Ruth 2:15 And when she had risen up to glean, Boaz commanded his young men saying, Let her glean even among the sheaves, and do not rebuke her.
2:16 And also let fall of the handfuls on purpose for her, and leave them so that she may glean them, and do not rebuke her. (MKJV)

Boaz waited until after Ruth had risen from the table to glean before he commanded the young men. He didn't want Ruth to know that he was giving her special treatment. *Let her glean even among the sheaves* was his command. He also told them to pull out handfuls of what they had reaped, and leave them for her to glean. Both commands were followed by the admonition, *and do not rebuke her*. Ruth had no idea of the personal harvest that she was about to bring in that day.

Imagine the fun it must have been for the reapers to do this. I suppose it might have turned into a playful kind of interaction, as Ruth began to notice what they were doing. There was likely some smiling and eye contact between Ruth and the young workers. And Boaz was behind it all. Boaz was secretly looking out for Ruth.

Jesus said something about doing good deeds in secret.

Matthew 6:3 But you doing merciful deeds, do not let your left know what your right hand does,
6:4 so that your merciful deeds may be in secret. And your Father seeing in secret Himself will repay you in the open. (LITV)

This story has surprises for everyone. Even Boaz is in for a surprise!

Proverbs 19:17 Whoever is generous to the poor lends to the LORD, and he will repay him for his deed. (ESV)

In this living parable, the master of the harvest commanded his reapers concerning Ruth. And as it was with Ruth, so it is with every recipient of the grace of God. He has commanded His angels concerning us. Who knows what *handfuls on purpose* we may have received without even knowing?

An Ephah of Barley

Ask, and it shall be given you

Matthew 7:7

Ruth 2:17 So she gleaned in the field until evening, and beat out that she had gleaned: and it was about an ephah of barley.
2:18 And she took it up, and went into the city: and her mother in law saw what she had gleaned: and she brought forth, and gave to her that she had reserved after she was sufficed.

Ruth was no lazy person. She worked hard that day, and will continue in the days ahead. Naomi must have been astonished at the sight of Ruth's personal harvest! That *ephah of barley* probably weighed over 30 pounds, or nearly a bushel by our standards. But that was not all. Ruth also brought Naomi a prepared meal! This is a double blessing! But Ruth has something else for Naomi. We are nearing the first climax.

Ruth 2:19 And her mother-in-law said to her, "Where did you glean today? And where have you worked? Blessed be the man who took notice of you." (ESV)

Naomi is asking, and she is about to receive. It is amazing what a word can do.

The Unveiling Word

Like golden apples set in silver is a word spoken at the right time.

Proverbs 25:11 (ISV)

Ruth 2:19 And her mother-in-law said to her, "Where did you glean today? And where have you worked? Blessed be the man who took notice of you." So she told her mother-in-law with whom she had worked and said, "The man's name with whom I worked today is Boaz." (ESV)

There are times when a word can make a world of difference. This particular word happened to be a *name*. We are at the first climax of this story.

Ruth 2:20 And Naomi said to her daughter-in-law, "May he be blessed by the LORD, whose kindness has not forsaken the living or the dead!" Naomi also said to her, "The man is a close relative of ours, one of our redeemers." (ESV)

"May he be blessed by the LORD, whose kindness has not forsaken the living or the dead!" There is something different about Naomi. She isn't bitter anymore. Not so very long ago, Naomi had other things to say concerning the LORD:

Ruth 1:21 I went out full, and the LORD hath brought me home again empty: why then call ye me Naomi, seeing the LORD hath testified against me, and the Almighty hath afflicted me?

Hearing the name of Boaz removed her bitterness. Hearing the name of Boaz replaced bitterness with joy and restored hope. Boaz is sort of like Jesus this way, because this is what the name of Jesus always does.

Hearing the name of Boaz was a surprise for Naomi, who then surprises us! For Boaz, she says, is one of the family *redeemers.* The Hebrew word Naomi used here is *goel.* Boaz is the *goel,* the kinsman-redeemer. This is the first appearance of *goel* in the book of Ruth, and here is where we learn how significant this Boaz really is.

Naomi is starting to see the hand of God working on her behalf. Yet we have already seen that God was at work in Naomi's family from the beginning. He who works all things according to His purpose brought Naomi close to His side, and through her suffering began the mighty work we have before us, where all things will be made new, and Christ is glorified throughout. This seems to be what He does all the time.

Although Naomi has passed from this life a very long time ago, she has never really stopped living. She is alive somewhere in God's kingdom. And I wonder what it must be like for her (indeed, and for her whole family), on this side of the cross, to look back and see how God used her and her family to reveal His glory in the midst of their suffering.

I suspect that He is still doing that with us.

The Dead

Can you perform wonders for the dead?

Psalm 88:10 (ISV)

Blessed be he of the LORD, who hath not left off his kindness to the living and to the dead. (Ruth 2: 20)

In the first chapter we read that Naomi's daughters-in-law kindly *dealt with the dead* (1:8). Here, we find that the LORD has not left off His *kindness* to the living *and to the dead*. Understanding this role of the dead is essential in recognizing the magnitude of the book of Ruth. Without *the dead*, there is no book of Ruth.

Death brought misery into their lives, as death always does; but the story does not end there (it never does, though we may feel like it does). This story of hope restored transcends hope for the living; for here we learn of a *redeemer*, and that the LORD has not left off His kindness to the living *and to the dead*.

Naomi has joy for knowledge of Boaz, the kinsman-redeemer, who is able to restore the *name* of the dead. How much more should our joy be full, knowing the *name* of Jesus, our true Redeemer; who has, and can, and will restore *life* to the dead!

John 11:25 Jesus said unto her, I am the resurrection, and the life: he that believeth in me, though he were dead, yet shall he live:

Not My Will

For I came down from heaven, not to do mine own will, but the will of him that sent me.

John 6:38

Ruth 2:21 And Ruth the Moabitess said, He said unto me also, Thou shalt keep fast by my young men, until they have ended all my harvest.

This passage seems to reveal something about Ruth; possibly by way of her human weakness. We have to understand that Ruth had no man in her life. She was a *young* widow. Loneliness can take a toll on anyone. Most of us desire companionship, particularly from the opposite sex. Ruth was no different. Notice again what she told Naomi: She said that Boaz told her to *keep fast by* the *young men*. Let's go back a few verses and see what Boaz really told her:

Ruth 2:8 Then said Boaz unto Ruth, Hearest thou not, my daughter? Go not to glean in another field, neither go from hence, but abide here fast by my maidens:

Boaz told her to stay by the maidens. But Ruth has a will of her own, and she has desires. Perhaps she might obtain a husband from among the young men. This is understandable, considering her situation. But Naomi has other plans for Ruth.

Ruth 2:22 And Naomi said unto Ruth her daughter in law, It is good, my daughter, that thou go out with his maidens, that they meet thee not in any other field.

Naomi understands that Ruth is a desirable young woman. She also knows that Boaz bestowed extraordinary kindness toward her. She knows that Boaz is their *goel*, their kinsman-redeemer. The hand of God is at work, and Naomi is doing her part in much the same way a farmer does his part when God brings the rain.

One of the things the farmer does is protect his crops from vermin.

 Naomi sees another kind of *harvest* on the horizon, but Ruth's emptiness and those servant boys might spoil it. She suggests that it would be good for her to stay with the young women.

And what does Ruth do?

Ruth 2:23 So she kept fast by the maidens of Boaz to glean unto the end of barley harvest and of wheat harvest; and dwelt with her mother in law.

Sometimes we think we know what we want. It is good to understand that our own feelings and desires are not always our best guides. Ruth honored her deceased husband's mother, whom she loved. She placed Naomi's concerns above her own life, and in doing so, put herself in a position to receive something far greater than the fleeting promises of her own feelings and desires. Ruth followed not her own will, but the will of her mother-in-law. Ruth is sort of like Jesus that way.[1]

---

[1] Some English translations do not recognize the gender distinction in this passage. See Appendix – *On Ruth's Desire to Work with the Young Men* at the end of this book.

Chapter 3

Seeking Rest

Come unto me, all ye that labour and are heavy laden …

Matthew 11:28

Ruth 3:1 Then Naomi her mother in law said unto her, My daughter, shall I not seek rest for thee, that it may be well with thee?
3:2 And now is not Boaz of our kindred, with whose maidens thou wast? Behold, he winnoweth barley to night in the threshingfloor.

It appears Naomi is in the habit of asking leading questions. She likely got that from Elimelech. It seems to run in his family. We find their kinsman Boaz doing the same thing: *Hearest thou not, my daughter? Have I not charged the young men that they shall not touch thee?* (Ruth 2:8, 9).

So Naomi does it too. Remember that other time she asked those leading questions? When the tears were running down her cheeks? (So here I am asking leading questions, too. I guess it runs in the Family.) Naomi asked her daughters-in-law if she had any sons for them. She asked that even if she was married and could conceive sons for them, would they wait until they were grown to marry them. The obvious answer to both questions was *No.* So here she goes again – but this time there are no tears. This time there is hope, with great anticipation. And this time, both answers are *Yes!*

Again, looking back to that other time, what was Naomi's concern for her daughters-in-law?

Ruth 1:9 The LORD grant you that ye may find rest, each of you in the house of her husband.

Rest is a settled state of comfort and quietness. It brings a feeling of security. And the idea conveyed both times by Naomi is that *rest* is found by a woman residing in the house of her husband.

The church is the bride of Christ. And Christ, our Bridegroom, promises *rest.* Naomi sought to help Ruth in finding rest in their redeemer. And we might do well in helping someone else to find rest in our Redeemer, Jesus Christ.

> *... and I will give you rest.*
>
> *Matthew 11:28*

.

Naomi's Turn

And the God of peace shall bruise Satan
under your feet shortly.

Romans 16:20

We are now at the end of two harvests. Ruth has been faithful to the end in remaining with the female workers. And Naomi has been patiently waiting for the right time to make her move. She knows that Boaz is a *goel*, a kinsman-redeemer, who is able to restore their family's name in Israel through marriage. She also knows that he has been very partial toward Ruth.

The time has come for winnowing barley; separating the good grain from the chaff. Boaz will be out on the threshing floor, where he will also be spending the night. For Naomi, this is the right time. She tells Ruth what she must do.

Ruth 3:3 Wash thyself therefore, and anoint thee, and put thy raiment upon thee, and get thee down to the floor: but make not thyself known unto the man, until he shall have done eating and drinking.
3:4 And it shall be, when he lieth down, that thou shalt mark the place where he shall lie, and thou shalt go in, and uncover his feet, and lay thee down; and he will tell thee what thou shalt do.

Naomi really thought this thing through! She probably spent hours on end, planning every detail while Ruth was out gleaning the fields. The devil had his little victory in Moab when Elimelech and his sons died there. But now it's Naomi's turn. Her day has arrived, and her plans are all in order. This battle will be decisive, and lost ground will be recovered. Don't you love how God gives His people a part in the victory?

Ruth had to be well dressed and smelling good. But this was not enough. To get the full and undivided attention of Boaz required some strategy. Ruth would have to go out on the threshing floor and spy on Boaz, ensuring that he did not see her. She was to watch him until he lay down to sleep. She would then approach him, uncover his feet and lay down. That would surely get his attention! To add to the surprise, Boaz would see Ruth, beautiful and fragrant, lying at his feet! Naomi was a very wise woman; a ranking general in the army of God.

The Feet of the Redeemer

… and thou shalt go in, and uncover his feet

Ruth 3:4

After Boaz lies down to sleep, Ruth is to approach him and uncover his feet. Then she is to lie down and wait for him to tell her to what do. This seems strange to us, being about three thousand years removed from that time and culture. So in order to more fully appreciate this *living parable,* we would do well to learn something of the significance of the *feet* in ancient Israel. We'll start at the feet of Jesus.

Luke 7:37 And, behold, a woman in the city, which was a sinner, when she knew that Jesus sat at meat in the Pharisee's house, brought an alabaster box of ointment,
7:38 And stood at his feet behind him weeping, and began to wash his feet with tears, and did wipe them with the hairs of her head, and kissed his feet, and anointed them with the ointment.

Here we find a woman who placed herself at the feet of Jesus, and washed His feet with her tears and some very expensive ointment, while wiping them with her hair. She also kissed His feet. Here is what Jesus said about her.

Luke 7:47 So I'm telling you that her sins, as many as they are, have been forgiven, and that's why she has shown such great love. But the one to whom little is forgiven loves little. (ISV)

According to Jesus, in her washing and kissing of His feet, this woman was showing *great love.* People do not do that today. This kind of activity is completely foreign to us in our time and culture. Had we no prior knowledge of this biblical reference, we would have some difficulty understanding someone doing that. But that is what this woman did. And Jesus commended her for it.

In another passage, a man named Jairus falls down at the feet of Jesus.

Luke 8:41 And, behold, there came a man named Jairus, and he was a ruler of the synagogue: and he fell down at Jesus' feet, and besought him that he would come into his house:

These days we are not in the habit of throwing ourselves down at the feet of other people, not even those we highly regard. We are so far removed from the times, places, and cultures that practiced such things it would not even enter our minds to do something like that. In fact, we would find it strange if we saw someone who did. But this is what Jairus did. He fell down at the feet of Jesus.

Jairus fell. Mary sat.

Luke 10:38 Now it came to pass, as they went, that he entered into a certain village: and a certain woman named Martha received him into her house.
10:39 And she had a sister called Mary, which also sat at Jesus' feet, and heard his word.

Mary sat at the feet of Jesus to hear His word. Martha was busy serving, and she was upset that Mary was not helping her. So she complained to Jesus. Here is what Jesus said to Martha.

Luke 10:41 And Jesus answered and said unto her, Martha, Martha, thou art careful and troubled about many things:
10:42 But one thing is needful: and Mary hath chosen that good part, which shall not be taken away from her.

In answering Martha, Jesus said that there is *one thing* which *is needful*. In other words, this *one thing* is necessary. He also called it *that good part,* and Mary had chosen it. This *one thing* would be sitting at His feet and hearing His word. He said it would *not be taken from her*. There appears to be a difference between Mary's perspective of Jesus, and Martha's. Martha became distracted with other things while serving, but Mary sat at His feet and learned of Him. Mary chose the *good part*.

And then there is this other instance when the tables were turned; that time when Jesus placed *Himself* at the feet of His own disciples.

John 13:3 Jesus knowing that the Father had given all things into his hands, and that he was come from God, and went to God;
13:4 He riseth from supper, and laid aside his garments; and took a towel, and girded himself.
13:5 After that he poureth water into a bason, and began to wash the disciples' feet, and to wipe them with the towel wherewith he was girded.

In ancient times, people wore sandals, walked everywhere, and their feet got dirty. They had to wash their feet. But it was also normal in those days for upper class people to have their feet washed by their servants; their slaves. In washing the feet of His disciples, Jesus exemplified something He had been teaching them:

Mark 10:42 And Jesus called them to him and said to them, "You know that those who are considered rulers of the Gentiles lord it over them, and their great ones exercise authority over them.

10:43 But it shall not be so among you. But whoever would be great among you must be your servant,
10:44 and whoever would be first among you must be slave of all.

Mark 10:45 For even the Son of Man came not to be served but to serve, and to give his life as a ransom for many." (ESV)

First He taught them. They spent years in His presence learning of Him. And when the time of His departure drew near, He showed them what He meant, by doing what He taught them. And He did it to *them*.

Remember that woman in Luke's gospel who washed His feet with her tears? Jesus said her sins were many, but they had been forgiven, which is why she had shown *great love*. And here is the sinless One, needing no one's forgiveness, placing *Himself* at the feet of sinful men. The Lord of lords and King of kings cast aside His garments, put on humility, and began a task relegated to slaves. He loved them that much.

From these examples, we see that placing one's self at the feet of another shows submission and humility. At the same time it also acknowledges something of value, worthiness or superiority toward the other person. We are now in a position to better understand what took place that night on the threshing floor.

Ruth's Response

And he saw also a certain poor widow....

Luke 21:2

Ruth 3:5 And she said unto her, All that thou sayest unto me I will do.

Naomi had given Ruth some very detailed instructions, which required a combination of boldness and humility. She was to approach this man, while in his bed (or whatever he used for a bed under the stars), uncover his feet and lay herself down there. Most of us might have some questions about that. We might even suggest some other ideas.

Without batting an eye, Ruth merely replied, "*All that thou sayest unto me I will do.*" Wow. Who wouldn't want someone like that? Interestingly, there was another time when all of Israel responded to God in very much the same way.

Exodus 19:7 And Moses came and called for the elders of the people, and laid before their faces all these words which the LORD commanded him. 19:8 and all the people answered together, and said, All that the LORD hath spoken we will do. And Moses returned the words of the people unto the LORD.

How many who made that statement actually kept the promise? Not one person in all human history kept all of God's commandments, with the exception of Jesus Christ. Without question, Jesus did the will of His Father. He was faithful unto death.

If Ruth could be marked by one character trait, it might be faithfulness. She fulfilled her promise, and her motivation was love for an old widow. When compared to great things some people have accomplished, this seems rather small and insignificant; a widow caring for a widow in a small village. We can be deceived by appearances.

Luke 21:1 And he looked up, and saw the rich men casting their gifts into the treasury.
21:2 And he saw also a certain poor widow casting in thither two mites.
21:3 And he said, Of a truth I say unto you, that this poor widow hath cast in more than they all:
21:4 For all these have of their abundance cast in unto the offerings of God: but she of her poverty hath cast in all the living that she had.

Jesus saw *a certain poor widow*; and her story has been told and retold for two thousand years. This person is in our Bibles, having received her place in the inspired Word.

And we are reading the story of an otherwise unknown family, whose men died. Their wives became widows. And out of death and despair, God elevates a young widow of a people not chosen; a widow, who served a widow. And through His providence she is honored in His story, with the title bearing her name. And we are studying her, and learning of Jesus. God is glorified through Ruth.

And he saw also a certain poor widow.

She Went Down

Let this mind be in you, which was also in Christ Jesus

Philippians 2:5

Ruth 3:6 And she went down unto the floor, and did according to all that her mother in law bade her.

In order to carry out her promise, Ruth had to descend. She had to go down. Lowering one's self is normally not a desirable thing. Yet it is a requirement. One who magnifies self cannot be said to be truly submitted to the Master.

Philippians 2:3 Do nothing from selfish ambition or conceit, but in humility count others more significant than yourselves. (ESV)

Ruth had proven faithful in smaller things, and now she is tested with a greater commitment. And we know that Ruth is faithful, and will be to the very end. She went down to the threshing floor.

Boaz is there, separating the good grain from the chaff. It is a lot of work, and he will also have his meal and spend the night there; most likely to protect his produce from animals and thieves. Do you suppose he had any idea that he was being watched? He was a marked man. Ruth set her sights on him. She watched, and waited patiently until he went to lie down. Then she made her move.

Entering into His Rest

Therefore, since the promise to enter his rest remains, let us beware that none of you be found to have fallen short.

Hebrews 4:1 (CSB)

Ruth 3:7 And when Boaz had eaten and drunk, and his heart was merry, he went to lie down at the end of the heap of grain: and she came softly, and uncovered his feet, and laid her down.

What Ruth did that night on the threshing floor, we all must do. There comes a time when we are all faced with that same decision: *Will we place ourselves at the feet of the Redeemer?* There is no other place for us to go. And it always involves a mix of fear, humility and boldness; along with the likelihood of rejection.

Jesus will never reject anyone who comes to Him; but your friends may reject you. Your family might reject you. You may have to change jobs. And in many places in the world, you can be arrested or even killed. The reality is that this world rejected Christ, and crucified Him. And it continues to reject Him by rejecting us. History hasn't changed. Salvation is a free gift, but it does have its cost.

Ruth placed herself at the feet of the redeemer. She literally entered into his rest. Unlike Jesus, who promises that He will never cast out anyone who comes to Him (John 6:37), Boaz is not the Son of God. He is completely human. As far as Ruth knew, he may not accept her. And a woman entering secretly into the bed of a man easily entails other negative consequences, which no one may ever know. These things happen. But those possibilities of rejection, or worse, did not stop Ruth. Nor should that keep us from Jesus Christ, our true Redeemer.

For we which have believed do enter into that rest (Hebrews 4:3)

A Woman Rejected

(a brief aside)

But he answered her not a word.

Matthew 15:23

We are told that Jesus will never reject anyone who comes to Him. But there *is* one story in the New Testament where Jesus actually *did* reject someone who came to Him for help. Or so it appears.

Matthew 15:22 And, behold, a woman of Canaan came out of the same coasts, and cried unto him, saying, Have mercy on me, O Lord, thou Son of David; my daughter is grievously vexed with a devil.
15:23 But he answered her not a word.

This woman came to Jesus in desperation on behalf of her daughter. But Jesus went about His business as if she was not even there. To make matters worse, His disciples tried to have her removed.

15:23 And his disciples came and besought him, saying, Send her away; for she crieth after us.

It appears that she was getting on everyone's nerves. She must have been loud and annoying. They wanted to get rid of her. And then Jesus Himself told her that he was not there to help her. Seems a bit cold, does it not?

15:24 But he answered and said, I am not sent but unto the lost sheep of the house of Israel.

This woman was rejected. She was not an Israelite. Jesus came to minister to the house of Israel, not her. She may have already known this, but that did not stop her. It gets worse.

Matthew 15:25 Then came she and worshipped him, saying, Lord, help me.

This woman is desperate. This is about her daughter! She throws herself at His feet and worships Him, pleading for help! Then He drops this bombshell:

Matthew 15:26 But he answered and said, It is not meet to take the children's bread, and to cast it to dogs.

Cast it to the dogs? What a horrible thing to say to a woman pleading for the life of her child! She is torn to the soul.

But what is Jesus *really* doing? He is teaching *us* through this wonderful, beautiful person. He knows exactly what to say, because He knows exactly how she will respond. Sometimes it is necessary for God to pull out of us what is inside of us; and it can hurt. But we would do well to pay attention and learn. This woman will not give up. But she knows her place. She is humble.

Matthew 15:27 And she said, Truth, Lord: yet the dogs eat of the crumbs which fall from their masters' table.

Even when it seems that He rejects us (but He is on our side), we should never stop seeking Him. God gives grace to the humble. As for this woman, Jesus heard her, and granted her request.

Matthew 15:28 Then Jesus answered and said unto her, O woman, great is thy faith: be it unto thee even as thou wilt. And her daughter was made whole from that very hour.

So what really happened here? Jesus took this seemingly random situation and demonstrated something that He had been teaching His disciples about prayer all along:

Luke 11:5 Then he told them, "Suppose one of you has a friend, and you go to him at midnight and say to him, 'Friend, let me borrow three loaves of bread.
11:6 A friend of mine on a trip has dropped in on me, and I don't have anything to serve him.'
11:7 Suppose he answers from inside, 'Stop bothering me! The door is already locked, and my children are here with us in the bedroom. I can't get up and give you anything!'
11:8 I tell you, even though that man doesn't want to get up and give him anything because he is his friend, he will get up and give him whatever he needs because of his persistence.
11:9 So I say to you: Keep asking, and it will be given you. Keep searching, and you will find. Keep knocking, and the door will be opened for you. (ISV)

Jesus has an interesting way of demonstrating the things He teaches. He did it when He washed the feet of His disciples, and He did it with this Canaanite woman. And if you pay attention, He is still doing it.

The Power of Love

…nevertheless not as I will, but as thou wilt.

Matthew 26:39

Ruth was humble. She did not go down to that threshing floor as some self-serving opportunist. She simply obeyed Naomi, and placed herself at the mercy of Boaz.

Ruth 3:7 And when Boaz had eaten and drunk, and his heart was merry, he went to lie down at the end of the heap of grain. Then she came softly and uncovered his feet and lay down.
3:8 At midnight the man was startled and turned over, and behold, a woman lay at his feet! (ESV)

If Boaz was asleep before, we can be sure that he didn't sleep a wink the rest of that night! We've reached the second climax. This one's for Boaz.

Ruth 3:9 And he said, Who art thou? And she answered, I am Ruth thine handmaid: spread therefore thy skirt over thine handmaid; for thou art a near kinsman.

Don't you love how God works? It may take an entire harvest (or even a millennium) before He moves; but when He does, He is quick! He leaves no time for gradual decisions. You are suddenly confronted with the truth, and have to decide. And here, Boaz suddenly finds a woman lying at his feet in the middle of the night; but not just any young woman. This was Ruth! And she is stunning! And she smells good too! And *she* is proposing marriage to *him*! And she tells him that he is a near kinsman (*goel* is the word she used), which means it is his duty to do so.

For Boaz, this was a no-brainer. It was probably better than a dream come true!

Ruth 3:10 And he said, Blessed be thou of the LORD, my daughter: for thou hast shewed more kindness in the latter end than at the beginning, inasmuch as thou followedst not young men, whether poor or rich.

Boaz is absolutely delighted! And he marks her kindness by not following after *the young men*. I wonder what Ruth may have been thinking when he told her that. Remember what she said to Naomi back at the beginning of the harvest?

Ruth 2:21 And Ruth the Moabitess said, He said unto me also, Thou shalt keep fast by my young men, until they have ended all my harvest.

Of course we know that wasn't quite what Boaz actually said. It seems to have been Ruth's desire to do exactly what Boaz praised her for *not* doing. Sounds like us, doesn't it? After all, Ruth is human. And who knows what interactions may have taken place on the fields when the young men supplied her with those *handfuls on purpose*? But her submission to Naomi, rather than doing her own will, won the blessing of the redeemer.

There was a time when Someone Else chose to set aside His own will to follow the will of Another.

Mark 14:35 And he went forward a little, and fell on the ground, and prayed that, if it were possible, the hour might pass from him. 14:36 And he said, Abba, Father, all things are possible unto thee; take away this cup from me: nevertheless not what I will, but what thou wilt.

Christ's submission to the Father's will won Him victory over death and hell, a Name above all names, brought salvation to the whole world, and far more than we can begin to comprehend. But there was this moment in time when His will was not the same as the will of the Father. He followed the Father's will. He loved us that much.

He also left us an example. So maybe the question is not so much about what you want to do or would rather not do, but who do you love, and how much?

Losing Life, and Finding It

Therefore I say unto you, Take no thought for your life,

Luke 12:22

Ruth gave up a possible future with a new husband when she left Moab to accompany Naomi. And the blessings began. She gave up the possibility of companionship with a young man she might grow to love when she placed Naomi's concern above her own desires. And the blessings never stopped flowing. And it gets better; but not without placing herself at the feet of the redeemer.

Ruth 3:11 And now, my daughter, fear not; I will do to thee all that thou requirest: for all the city of my people doth know that thou art a virtuous woman.
3:12 And now it is true that I am thy near kinsman: howbeit there is a kinsman nearer than I.

Boaz says, "*Yes!*" And he backs that up by telling her that *all the city* knows that she is a *virtuous woman*! This was long before Proverbs 31 was written (but you can learn more about the virtuous woman there, beginning at verse 10). This is quite a compliment. And with Ruth, it's also very true.

So that was the good news. But there is also *other* news. There is another man who is a closer kinsman than Boaz. We will never know if this was *bad* news. That other fellow might have made a fine husband for Ruth. Of course, this is an old story and we already know how it ends. But the entrance of this other person is the perfect ingredient in bringing out a taste of the character of Boaz.

All those days working the fields, Boaz had ample opportunity to move closer to Ruth, and could have easily won her affection. He was, after all, a mighty man of wealth and honor. What woman would not want a man like that? But Boaz was also a *godly* man. You don't find many of those.

Boaz knew that this other man came before him in the order of kinsman. He could not marry Ruth on the basis of his own desire for love and companionship without violating this long-established order. It might also lead to some measure of contempt; either by this other kinsman, or someone else. Contempt and ill feelings have a way of getting around. Boaz was above that. He denied himself.

And again, Ruth was a younger woman. And what is more natural than for her to fall in love and marry someone closer to her own age? Boaz would not, for his own selfish motive, stand in the way of fulfilling her desire for a fine young man her age. In his response to Ruth, that she did not follow after the young men (v. 10), Boaz seems to give away that rationale.

And so Boaz, while favoring Ruth throughout the harvest with *handfuls on purpose* (in secret through his reapers), which Ruth in turn, provided for Naomi, did not interfere with her freedom to make her own choices. And now she is at *his* feet, proposing marriage to *him*; yet for the sake of *Naomi*.

And so we have two people, who, in setting aside their own personal lives and desires for the sake of others, are brought together. And even this is not of their doing, but by the will of someone else. I don't think they are disappointed.

But there *is* this other kinsman. It's not over yet.

Tarrying at His Feet

When thou liest down, thou shalt not be afraid

Proverbs 3:24

Ruth 3:13 Tarry this night, and it shall be in the morning, that if he will perform unto thee the part of a kinsman, well; let him do the kinsman's part: but if he will not do the part of a kinsman to thee, then will I do the part of a kinsman to thee, as the LORD liveth: lie down until the morning.
3:14 And she lay at his feet until the morning:

Note the humility of the redeemer. He certainly desires Ruth! And yet, there is one who is before him in line to fulfill the part of the kinsman. Boaz is willing to wait, and take the chance of losing her to someone else, to do the right thing.

He tells Ruth to tarry for the night. Until Boaz learns what this nearer kinsman decides, he won't touch her. In spite of what some scholars and commentators have imagined, nothing scandalous happened that night on the threshing floor. Ruth remained *at his feet until morning*. You have God's Word on that.

Entering into his rest, Ruth remained at the feet of the redeemer for the night. The morning is coming, and he will rise and take care of business. They will be together again as bride and bridegroom. We know how it ends. But for now, she must tarry the night.

And we know that we also will be with our Bridegroom. We have His Word. We know how it ends. But for now, we must tarry the night as well.

The Secret

And he charged them that they should tell no man of him.

Mark 8:30

Ruth 3:14 And she lay at his feet until the morning: and she rose up before one could know another. And he said, Let it not be known that a woman came into the floor.

It is early morning, not yet light. The proposal has been made and conditionally accepted. Today Boaz will meet with this other kinsman and discuss the matter. He was probably awake the whole night thinking of ways to tip the odds in his favor. For now, it is still dark. No one knows one from another. And Boaz wants to keep it that way. Word must not get out that *a woman came into the floor*. We can be sure that Boaz has a strategy, and it seems keeping Ruth's midnight visit a secret was crucial for the success of his plan.

Boaz is sort of like Jesus this way, for Christ also had a strategy. He knew why He came. He knew what He had to do. And He knew there were some things that needed to remain secret, and for good reason.

1st Corinthians 2:7 But we speak the wisdom of God in a mystery, even the hidden wisdom, which God ordained before the world unto our glory:
2:8 Which none of the princes of this world knew: for had they known it, they would not have crucified the Lord of glory.

Waiting for the Redeemer

Looking for that blessed hope

Titus 2:13

It is no secret to us that Boaz desires Ruth and is working on a plan that might hopefully bring them together. He wants to keep a lid on her visit the night before. If news of that got out, it might have a negative effect. He sends her back into town before daylight, but not without a gift for Naomi.

Ruth 3:15 And he said, "Bring the garment you are wearing and hold it out." So she held it, and he measured out six measures of barley and put it on her. Then she went into the city.
3:16 And when she came to her mother-in-law, she said, "How did you fare, my daughter?" Then she told her all that the man had done for her,
3:17 saying, "These six measures of barley he gave to me, for he said to me, 'You must not go back empty-handed to your mother-in-law.'"
3:18 She replied, "Wait, my daughter, until you learn how the matter turns out, for the man will not rest but will settle the matter today." (ESV)

Boaz fully understood Naomi's hand in sending Ruth to the threshing floor that night; for how else would Ruth, a Moabite, have known of his role as *goel* (kinsman-redeemer) in Israel? But Naomi knew. And so Boaz sent her the gift of six measures of barley by Ruth's hand. Naomi got the message. She understood the gift. And now they must *wait*.

Chapter 4

Boaz Prevails

He who overcomes, I will make him a pillar in the temple of My God.

Revelation 3:12 (NKJV)

Ruth 4:1 Boaz went to the town gate and took a seat there. Just then the family redeemer he had mentioned came by, so Boaz called out to him, "Come over here and sit down, friend. I want to talk to you." So they sat down together.
4:2 Then Boaz called ten leaders from the town and asked them to sit as witnesses. (NLT)

The gate of the city was the place where the people came and went. It was also the equivalent to our modern courts of law, or town squares. It is here that the decision will be made regarding Ruth.

Boaz gives this other man no time to plan or scheme. He calls the man and gathers the elders. This will happen quickly. His strategy is two-fold: good news and *other* news; with hope that this *other* news might work to his advantage. So he starts with the good news.

Ruth 4:3 And he said unto the kinsman, Naomi, that is come again out of the country of Moab, selleth a parcel of land, which was our brother Elimelech's:
4:4 And I thought to advertise thee, saying, Buy it before the inhabitants, and before the elders of my people. If thou wilt redeem it, redeem it: but if thou wilt not redeem it, then tell me, that I may know: for there is none to redeem it beside thee; and I am after thee. And he said, I will redeem it.

The good news is that there is land for sale. Naomi is the seller, and since this man is the closest kinsman to Elimelech, he is first in line to buy it. Everything is set. The elders are present, and if he is not interested, Boaz wants to know, because he is next in line after him.

Upon hearing this seemingly good news, the man says he will redeem it. He will buy the land. And now, Boaz will present phase two of his strategy; the *other* news.

Ruth 4:5 Then Boaz said, "The day you buy the field from the hand of Naomi, you also acquire Ruth the Moabite, the widow of the dead, in order to perpetuate the name of the dead in his inheritance." (ESV)

This poor fellow is put on the spot in front of ten witnesses first thing in the morning. It's one thing to buy a piece of land. The man was ready to do that. But then Boaz begins to explain the arrangement. The elders are watching. Boaz unfolds the package deal; about acquiring *Ruth the Moabite, the widow of the dead, in order to perpetuate the name of the dead in his inheritance.* There is no mistaking the implication, and this poor guy is probably looking a little sick at this point. The elders were likely smiling. Is he going to acquire a Moabite wife right now before ten witnesses? This is too early and too sudden. He would have certainly bought the land, but marrying a Moabite woman was not even a consideration. What began as a good deal doesn't seem so good after all. He has other things to do today, and he will get along just fine without buying that land. He chooses the path of least resistance.

Ruth 4:6 And the kinsman said, I cannot redeem it for myself, lest I mar mine own inheritance: redeem thou my right to thyself; for I cannot redeem it.

Concerned for his *own inheritance*, this other kinsman chose not to redeem. Left up to him, the name of the dead would remain dead. Though he owned the power to restore it, he was driven by other concerns; his own concerns. We might say that he sought to save his life, rather than lose it. And this is the last we see of him. But Boaz will receive a place of special honor.

Let's jump ahead about two hundred years, to a different threshing floor, about six miles north of Bethlehem, where a major building project is taking place. The man in charge here is also the chief architect. His name is Hiram. Hiram is working under the commission of none other than King Solomon, and the building will soon become the temple of God.

History will remember it as Solomon's Temple. This is the place where God will cause His name to dwell. Here, heaven will touch the earth. God will meet with man in its inner chamber, the Holy of Holies. Sin will be atoned for, and many offerings will be sacrificed. This will be a place of great feasts and celebration in the presence of God. Solomon received the plans for it from his father, King David; who told him that he received its design from God's hand upon him; every detail (1st Chron. 28:19).

Standing in front of the temple as it is being built, we are facing westward. Towering nearly thirty feet above us, two bronze pillars have just been placed at its entrance. Hiram made those. And he gave them names, as instructed in the pattern given by the hand of God upon David.

2nd Chronicles 3:17 *And he reared up the pillars before the temple, one on the right hand, and the other on the left; and called the name of that on the right hand Jachin, and the name of that on the left Boaz.*

The Sandal

And if the man like not to take his brother's wife,

Deuteronomy 25:7

Ruth 4:7 And this was the custom in former times in Israel concerning redeeming and concerning changing, to confirm everything. A man plucked off his sandal and gave it to his neighbor. And this was a testimony in Israel.
4:8 Therefore the kinsman said to Boaz, Buy it for yourself. So he drew off his sandal. (MKJV)

By the time that the book of Ruth was written, this custom of the sandal was no longer practiced, so it is given a brief explanation here in the text. But the tradition is also found in the book of the Law. In Deuteronomy, the *sandal* is part of an additional instruction in the event that one refused to marry his brother's wife.

Deuteronomy 25:7 But if the man does not desire to take his brother's wife, then his brother's wife shall go up to the gate to the elders and say, 'My husband's brother refuses to establish a name for his brother in Israel; he is not willing to perform the duty of a husband's brother to me.'
25:8 Then the elders of his city shall summon him and speak to him. And if he persists and says, 'I do not desire to take her,'
25:9 then his brother's wife shall come to him in the sight of the elders, and pull his sandal off his foot and spit in his face; and she shall declare, 'Thus it is done to the man who does not build up his brother's house.' 25:10 In Israel his name shall be called, 'The house of him whose sandal is removed.' (NASB)

It was considered honorable in Israel for a man to marry his brother's widow and restore the name of his deceased brother. This was comparable to restoring life from the dead. The name that was lost in the death of the man without a son was restored by his brother through the wife of the man who died. This was expected.

The brother who refused to marry his brother's widow was in essence refusing to restore the name of his deceased brother. This was considered a disgrace, and was reflected by the public removal of *his sandal* by *his brother's wife,* who also *spit in his face* in the presence of the elders. The name of his *house* was also dishonored.

Deuteronomy grants the widow the legal right to remove the man's sandal. She would gain the sandal as a token before the elders, and likely retained ownership of her deceased husband's property, and be free to marry outside of his family. But this was not the desired outcome for a woman in that culture.

Here in the book of Ruth, Boaz stands in the place of the widow, who is Naomi. He is interceding on her behalf. Because she is past the age of childbearing, Ruth will be the bride through whom the name of the dead will be resurrected. Unlike Deuteronomy, here the kinsman removes his own sandal and hands it to Boaz. This is a transaction between redeemers. Boaz is both intercessor (for Naomi) and redeemer. There will be no losers in this transaction. It is merely a matter of who the redeemer is going to be. And so the closer relative removes his own sandal and hands it over to Boaz, thereby granting his right and responsibility to his next of kin. Boaz now owns the right to redeem.

The reason for using a *sandal* in this transaction has been lost. Today, opinions differ among scholars as to what the sandal represents. Two things are evident. The man who loses one of his sandals indicates loss on his part. At the same time, it signifies a kind of advantage by the gaining party over the losing party. Whatever the case, maybe it is enough for us to know that a sandal was used; and that it played a role in redemption.

About a thousand years later, John the Baptist will say something about a sandal; the sandal of another Redeemer, who is also our Intercessor, and our Bridegroom. Do you suppose there is a connection?

John 1:26 John answered them, saying, I baptize with water, but One stands among you whom you do not know.
1:27 He it is who, coming after me, who has been before me; of whom I am not worthy to loosen the thong of His sandal. (MKJV)

Day of Redemption

For ye are bought with a price

1st Corinthians 6:20

Ruth 4:9 And Boaz said unto the elders, and unto all the people, Ye are witnesses this day, that I have bought all that was Elimelech's, and all that was Chilion's and Mahlon's, of the hand of Naomi.
4:10 Moreover Ruth the Moabitess, the wife of Mahlon, have I purchased to be my wife, to raise up the name of the dead upon his inheritance, that the name of the dead be not cut off from among his brethren, and from the gate of his place: ye are witnesses this day.

We can picture Boaz holding that sandal high as he makes the announcement, which begins and ends with the words, *ye are witnesses this day!* And so they were. Everyone present that day witnessed to the fact that Boaz had bought and legally obtained from Naomi all that belonged to Elimelech and his sons. This included Ruth. Boaz *purchased* Ruth to be his wife, *to raise up the name of the dead upon his inheritance.*

In our time and culture, we find it unacceptable that a man *purchase* a wife. But that's what happened. And it couldn't have happened any other way; because that's what Jesus did. But we must not oversimplify this. Boaz did what the other kinsman was not willing to do. He indeed made a sacrifice in giving his life for Ruth. And Jesus Christ gave His life for us.

1st Peter 1:18 knowing that you were not redeemed with corruptible things, silver or gold, from your vain manner of life handed down from your fathers,
1:19 but with the precious blood of Christ (MKJV)

The Seed of the Woman

it shall bruise thy head

Genesis 3:15

Ruth 4:11 And all the people that were in the gate, and the elders, said, We are witnesses. The LORD make the woman that is come into thine house like Rachel and like Leah, which two did build the house of Israel: and do thou worthily in Ephratah, and be famous in Bethlehem:
4:12 And let thy house be like the house of Pharez, whom Tamar bare unto Judah, of the seed which the LORD shall give thee of this young woman.

The people and the elders acknowledged their witness of all that Boaz had just announced, making this transaction complete and legal. And then they began to bless Ruth and Boaz; that the LORD would make Ruth like the matriarchs of Israel, *Rachel and Leah*; and that Boaz would *do worthily in Ephratah, and be famous in Bethlehem*. But it doesn't stop there. The blessing continues to include the *house* of Boaz; *thy house*. They're speaking of the future generations of his family; that his *house* would *be like the house of Pharez.*

Pharez was Boaz's great, great, great, great grandfather, who also had a lot of other descendants that made up entire towns and villages in Israel. They were called the Pharzites (Numbers 26:20). And so the people and the elders blessed Boaz with the intent that his house (his descendants) would be like that of Pharez. And God fulfilled this blessing, in more ways than one.

When the people and the elders referred to Pharez, they also happened to mention his parents, Tamar and Judah. Like Ruth, Tamar is also a champion in the ongoing war between seed and serpent. Her story is found in Genesis 37. I've dedicated a section for her in the Appendix. Our God is an awesome God.

The last phrase in this blessing warrants special attention.

... of the seed which the LORD shall give thee of this young woman. (v. 12)

Resting in the middle of this phrase is a statement of promise. *The LORD shall give thee.* This is a promise to Boaz. It leaves no room for doubt: *shall give*. This is something that the *LORD* is going to do. This will happen.

The words surrounding this promise tell us what the LORD will give to Boaz: *the seed... of this young woman*. The *LORD shall give* to Boaz the seed of this young woman; *the seed of the woman*. And He did.

Ruth opened with a victory for the devil; three dead, no seed. But the story did not end there. It ends here, with a new beginning, and restored hope.

And we're still not finished.

The New Birth

For unto you is born this day ....

Luke 2:11

Ruth 4:13 So Boaz took Ruth, and she became his wife. And he went in to her, and the LORD gave her conception, and she bore a son.

Boaz and Ruth are finally together. That night on the threshing floor produced far more than good grain for Boaz. It makes one wonder. For if this living parable of redemption provides a picture of what Jesus was going to do for us, does it not also provide something for Him? Are all parables only for our benefit? Or is something more going on?

As promised, the *LORD gave* Ruth *conception, and she bore a son.*

Ruth 4:14 Then the women said to Naomi, "Blessed be the LORD, who has not left you this day without a redeemer, and may his name be renowned in Israel! 4:15 He shall be to you a restorer of life and a nourisher of your old age, for your daughter-in-law who loves you, who is more to you than seven sons, has given birth to him." (ESV)

Did you catch that? They said, "*Blessed be the LORD, who has not left you this day without a redeemer.*" And then they said, "*For your daughter-in-law who loves you, who is more to you than seven sons, has given birth to him.*" They're talking about the baby. The baby is the *goel. He* is the redeemer. There seems to have been a transfer from father to son. Boaz was the *goel*, the kinsman-redeemer. His work is finished, and now their hope is in the *son*; the newborn babe. He is the redeemer.

And he was born in Bethlehem.

The Virtuous Woman

Who can find a virtuous woman?
for her price is far above rubies.

Proverbs 31:10

Ruth 4:14 And the women said unto Naomi, Blessed be the LORD, which hath not left thee this day without a kinsman, that his name may be famous in Israel.
4:15 And he shall be unto thee a restorer of thy life, and a nourisher of thine old age: for thy daughter in law, which loveth thee, which is better to thee than seven sons, hath born him.
4:16 And Naomi took the child, and laid it in her bosom, and became nurse unto it.

This is one happy occasion! We can picture Naomi glowing as she holds the baby close to her heart, with the neighbor women all together and sharing the joy of the moment. Ruth is there, and occupies a place of special recognition. In her unyielding *faith*fulness to Naomi, Ruth became the source of *hope* through her marriage to Boaz, now fulfilled in the birth of this child. And here, she is honored because of her *love* for Naomi.

1st Corinthians 13:13 And now abide faith, hope, love, these three; but the greatest of these is love. (NKJV)

Restorer of Life

He restoreth my soul

Psalm 23:3

Ruth 4:15 And he shall be unto thee a restorer of thy life, and a nourisher of thine old age: for thy daughter in law, which loveth thee, which is better to thee than seven sons, hath born him.

Father and son; both are redeemers. And the son shall be for Naomi a *restorer of life*. Is that not what Jesus is for us? Are we not like Naomi, whose name means *My Delight?* God loves us, and has redeemed us by His Son. Jesus, who is our Redeemer, continually restores our lives. And He continues to *nourish* us, even in our old age; for He is the Bread of Life. And with Jesus, it does not end. He is a restorer of life in more ways than one.

Jesus said unto her, I am the resurrection, and the life: he that believeth in me, though he were dead, yet shall he live: - John 11:25

The Day of Small Things

For unto us a child is born, unto us a son is given

Isaiah 9:6

Ruth 4:17 And the women her neighbours gave it a name, saying, There is a son born to Naomi; and they called his name Obed: he is the father of Jesse, the father of David.

And the women her neighbours gave it a name. Few people in the Bible were given names by someone other than their parents. We read in Scripture that God has done this on several occasions (Gen. 17:19; Isaiah 8:3; Hosea 1:4, 6 to name a few). His angels have done it (Gen. 16:11; Luke 1:13). But this occasion is unique in that the name of this child was given by *the women*, Naomi's *neighbours*; making this an extraordinarily special event.

It helps to understand the low status of women in that day to grasp this. And then you have to know Jesus to grasp its significance. Women in those days were often considered on the same level as property, and it was not out of the ordinary for a female to be bought, sold or traded. That level of social status is uncomfortably close to zero, which actually makes for a perfect fit in the wisdom of God.

1st Corinthians 1:28 God has chosen what is insignificant and despised in the world--what is viewed as nothing (CSB)

The lowly status of women in the Bible brings with it a special promise of greatness.

For he who is least among you all, he shall be great. (Luke 9:48)

This child was born of a poor young widow whose life was defined by serving her mother-in-law; a poor older widow. And he was named by the neighbor women, the least among the people of that day.

I suppose men of science have learned something of the power of small things when they opened up the atom. And we are learning something of the power of God in the small things.

There is a son born to Naomi;

From the beginning, Ruth has been setting her own life aside to care of Naomi. We might say that Ruth has been a living sacrifice; a sort of pre-fulfilling of Romans 12:1. And finally, here at the end of the story, she bears a son to Naomi; her only son. And he's the redeemer. Ruth is sort of like God this way; because that's what He did for us.

John 3:16 For God so loved the world, that he gave his only begotten Son, that whosoever believeth in him should not perish, but have everlasting life.

And they called his name Obed. Ruth bore this child to Naomi to resurrect the name of Elimelech, Naomi's deceased husband. Yet the women named him after Ruth, who served Naomi; for *Obed* means *serving*. He is the redeemer and the heir to all that pertains to Elimelech (*God is King*), and his name is *Serving*. Do you see Jesus?

Mark 10:45 For even the Son of Man did not come to be served, but to serve, and to give His life as a ransom for many. (LITV)

The Coming King

... yea, even in his kingdom he was born poor.

Ecclesiastes 4:14 (ASV)

Ruth 4:18 Now these are the generations of Pharez:
Pharez begat Hezron,
4:19 And Hezron begat Ram, and Ram begat
Amminadab, 4:20 And Amminadab begat Nahshon,
and Nahshon begat Salmon,
4:21 And Salmon begat Boaz, and Boaz begat Obed,
4:22 And Obed begat Jesse, and Jesse begat David.

Ruth provides the genealogy for King David. And though it was written after the fact, we can easily get a sense from the *story's* perspective that this genealogy looks both backward and forward in time. In that perspective, from the standpoint of the narrative and the people living within it, it points forward to David as the *coming* king, who will reign over Israel.

And this is exactly what we have seen throughout the whole story. Opening in famine and death, it closes with a harvest, a wedding and a new birth. From the man whose name means *God is King* to the baby born in Bethlehem who is called *Serving*; from *Weakness* to *Strength*, from death to life, from sorrow to celebration and a coming king, *Ruth* is a story that has Jesus Christ woven into its very fabric.

But that message can never be seen or realized apart from the cross. Without the cross, it simply is not there. But because of Christ, because of the cross, it *is* there. And we *can* see it. And this is also our assurance for the hope that we have in Him. We *see* Jesus. And as the name, Naomi, means *My Delight*, we too can be called Naomi; for we are *His delight*.

And we have learned in this living parable, this wonderful story of loss, love, sacrifice, and restoration, that God loves us and *is* working all things for our good; even when our whole world seems to be falling apart.

The Assembly of the LORD

The book of the genealogy of Jesus Christ, the son of David, the son of Abraham.

Matthew 1:1

Deuteronomy 23:3 "No Ammonite or Moabite may enter the assembly of the LORD. Even to the tenth generation, none of them may enter the assembly of the LORD forever," (ESV)

We saw this passage before. There are several interpretations among scholars as to what it meant to *not enter the assembly of the LORD.* But there *is* this assembly:

Matthew 1:2 Abraham was the father of Isaac, and Isaac the father of Jacob, and Jacob the father of Judah and his brothers,
1:3 and Judah the father of Perez and Zerah by Tamar, and Perez the father of Hezron, and Hezron the father of Ram,
1:4 and Ram the father of Amminadab, and Amminadab the father of Nahshon, and Nahshon the father of Salmon,
1:5 and Salmon the father of Boaz by Rahab, and Boaz the father of Obed by Ruth, (ESV)

This is the first section of the genealogy of Jesus Christ in Matthew's gospel. And this is the order of that genealogy: Abraham, Isaac, Jacob, Judah, Perez, Hezron, Aram, Amminadab, Nahshon, and Salmon. That's ten generations in this *assembly of the Lord;* or *assembling* of names in the genealogy of Jesus Christ, who is Lord. And as true as God is to His Word, there will be no Moabite found there. But look who made it in at number eleven:

… and Boaz the father of Obed by Ruth

Appendix

On the Use of Multiple Translations

I have several reasons for using different English Bible translations in this work. The primary reason is that the King James translation of 1611 is archaic, and many of its words and phrases have not been in use for well over a century, making understanding difficult for the modern reader.

That said, there are copyright limitations on nearly all of the modern Bible translations, thus restricting the amount of verses one can use without requiring further permissions beyond merely crediting the sources. I have tried to keep within those restrictions. And as much as possible, I used other English translations that are available in the public domain.

Maintaining the integrity of the original Hebrew has also played a part in selecting a proper translation (as the case with the male and female servants – see *On Ruth's Desire to Work with the Young Men* in this Appendix).

 Lastly, word order and phraseology are crucial in holding a reader's interest. Many of the verses used come from translations that, in my opinion, read well and say it best, while still adhering to the meaning of the original language.

Meanings of the Names

The meanings of the names, such as Boaz, Bethlehem, Elimelech, etc., these can be found in the following sources:

Brown-Driver-Briggs Hebrew and English Lexicon (BDB)
Fausset's Bible Dictionary

Strong's Exhaustive Concordance (Hebrew Dictionary)

Hitchcock Bible Dictionary

On Ruth's Desire to Work with the Young Men

On verses 2:21 and 2:22, some of the major translations (NIV, NASB, NLT and others) make no distinction of sex here, and have Ruth merely saying that Boaz told her to stay close to his servants. But the Hebrew is specific, and the distinction is clear. Without this information, we lose Ruth as a human being with personal desires, yet submitting to Naomi in spite of her desires. The following are the two Hebrew words used in the story. The definitions below are from the *Brown-Driver-Briggs Hebrew Lexicon.*

נער
na'ar
BDB Definition:
1) a boy, lad, servant, youth, retainer
1a) boy, lad, youth
1b) servant, retainer

נערה
na'ărâh
BDB Definition:
1) girl, damsel, female servant
1a) girl, damsel, little girl

In Ruth 2:8, Boaz told Ruth to abide close by his maidens (na'arah). In 2:21, Ruth told Naomi that Boaz told her to keep fast by his young men (na'ar). In 2:22, Naomi told Ruth to stay with his maidens (na'arah). In 2:23 Ruth worked with the maidens (na'arah) until the end of the harvest.

On uncovering the feet of Boaz

There are a lot of ideas floating around about what it meant to uncover the feet of Boaz, many of which imply sexual activity. Some reason that the word, "feet" may be a euphemism for a man's private part. But the problem with theories that lean in that direction is that the Bible does not hide the truth.

There is never any mistaking sexual activity wherever it is recorded in Scripture. Whether it is Lot's daughters in the cave with their father, Onan and Tamar, Judah and Tamar, Potiphar's wife and Joseph, Amnon and Tamar, the Song of Solomon, and too many other instances mention, the use of sexual terminology is not lacking in the Word of God.

It would be outside the integrity of Scripture to make an exception to this rule of straightforward raw honesty by which the Bible is known and trusted. It is, however, very common and very human to read into Scripture ideas we take in from the world around us. Of course, near the end of the story, we do find that Boaz went in unto Ruth, and God gave her conception (Ruth 4:13). So sexual activity did occur, but after they were married.

About Hiram

Hiram is the man who was in charge of building Solomon's temple. He made the two pillars and gave them their names, according to the instructions by the hand of God upon David. He was from Tyre. The people of Tyre were not Israelites. They worshiped other gods. So why would Solomon select this man from Tyre to oversee the building of God's temple? God probably told him to do that. As in all things, God knows what He is doing; and has not left us uninformed. And if you've been paying attention, God favors widows. He also seems partial to certain mixed marriages.

1st Kings 7:13 And King Solomon sent and brought Hiram out of Tyre.
7:14 He was the son of a widow woman of the tribe of Naphtali, and his father a man of Tyre, an engraver in bronze. And he was filled with the wisdom and understanding and knowledge to do all work in bronze. And he came to King Solomon and did all his work.
7:15 And he formed the two pillars of bronze; (ISV)

We just finished reading the book of Ruth, a story about widows. And Hiram was the son of a widow from the tribe of Naphtali. He was the perfect man for the job.

On the Pillar named Jachin

1ˢᵗ Kings 7:21 And he set up the pillars in the porch of the temple: and he set up the right pillar, and called the name thereof Jachin: and he set up the left pillar, and called the name thereof Boaz.

Jachin was the name of the other pillar Hiram made. It is also the name of another man of Israel. He was the fourth son of Simeon (Gen. 46:10). He had a lot of descendants, known as the Jachinites (Num. 26:12). But aside from these references, we know nothing about Jachin. And yet, God had instructed that the name of one of the two pillars of His temple be Jachin. We saw what Jesus said in Revelation:

Revelation 3:12 Him that overcometh will I make a pillar in the temple of my God

We don't know why God honored the name of Jachin on one of the pillars of His temple. But He did. God took note of Jachin. We will very likely hear more about him; later. But you have to know Jesus first in order for that to happen. There are people we never read about or hear about here on earth, who have stories as great as, or possibly greater than the ones found in our Bibles. And God is still writing His story into our lives.

Tamar

Tamar's story begins in Genesis 38. She was a Canaanite and the daughter-in-law of Judah. And she is one amazing woman. She occupies the ground of another field of battle in this war of seed and serpent. Her story began with two dead, and no seed. Both of the men who died were her husbands. After their deaths, she remained a childless widow for years. This is our first known reference point where a man was to marry his brother's widow in order to *raise up seed* for his deceased brother.

Genesis 38:6 And Judah took a wife for Er his firstborn, whose name was Tamar.
38:7 And Er, Judah's firstborn, was wicked in the sight of the LORD; and the LORD slew him.
38:8 And Judah said unto Onan, Go in unto thy brother's wife, and marry her, and raise up seed to thy brother.
38:9 And Onan knew that the seed should not be his; and it came to pass, when he went in unto his brother's wife, that he spilled it on the ground, lest that he should give seed to his brother.
38:10 And the thing which he did displeased the LORD: wherefore he slew him also.

Judah had arranged for his first son, Er, to marry young Tamar. But Er *was wicked in the sight of the LORD; and the LORD slew him* (38:7). We don't know what Er did, but it must have been really, really bad. The end result was that Tamar no longer had a husband. *Onan,* Er's brother, had the potential to be the first *goel* (kinsman-redeemer) in the Bible. But He refused to honor his father and fulfill his duty to Tamar.

What Onan did was likely more than a one-time event; and it was cruel. It says that the LORD *slew him also*.

In case you haven't noticed, the Lord still does that today. He does it in His church with His people. He did it to Ananias and Sapphira (Acts 5:1-10). And Paul had to explain to the people at the church in Corinth that God was doing it to them.

1st Corinthians 11:30 That is why many of you are weak and ill, and some have died.
11:31 But if we judged ourselves truly, we would not be judged.
11:32 But when we are judged by the Lord, we are disciplined so that we may not be condemned along with the world. (ESV)

God reserves the right to judge His people, and physical death is never the final word on any of us who belong to Him. This life is temporal. The next one is the one that counts. It is forever.

Getting back to Tamar's story:

Genesis 38:11 Then said Judah to Tamar his daughter in law, Remain a widow at thy father's house, till Shelah my son be grown: for he said, Lest peradventure he die also, as his brethren did. And Tamar went and dwelt in her father's house.

Judah never fulfilled his promise to Tamar. Shelah grew up. That takes years. And the years went by; and Judah either forgot all about Tamar, or deliberately avoided giving his other son to her. All we know is that Judah was not good with his promise.

Genesis 38:12 And in process of time the daughter of Shuah Judah's wife died; and Judah was comforted, and went up unto his sheepshearers to Timnath, he and his friend Hirah the Adullamite. 38:13 And it was told Tamar, saying, Behold thy father in law goeth up to Timnath to shear his sheep.

Genesis 38:14 And she put her widow's garments off from her, and covered her with a vail, and wrapped herself, and sat in an open place, which is by the way to Timnath; for she saw that Shelah was grown, and she was not given unto him to wife.

38:15 When Judah saw her, he thought her to be an harlot; because she had covered her face.

Tamar targeted Judah. He had promised her a son to give her seed in order to carry on the name of her deceased husband. Judah owed her that. We should be cautious in how we approach what Tamar did as it relates to our understanding of sexual immorality. She owned a legal right which was hers by promise. God sees that. Tamar was also a widow; twice. And God has a special place in His heart for widows.

Proverbs 15:25 The LORD will destroy the house of the proud: but he will establish the border of the widow.

The LORD saw Tamar being neglected for all those years. Judah, on the other hand, is a different story. His intent was purely sexual, which is why he went in and had sex with a woman he thought to be a harlot.

Genesis 38:16 He turned to her at the roadside and said, "Come, let me come in to you," for he did not know that she was his daughter-in-law. She said, "What will you give me, that you may come in to me?"

38:17 He answered, "I will send you a young goat from the flock." And she said, "If you give me a pledge, until you send it—"

38:18 He said, "What pledge shall I give you?" She replied, "Your signet and your cord and your staff that is in your hand." So he gave them to her and went in to her, and she conceived by him.

38:19 Then she arose and went away, and taking off her veil she put on the garments of her widowhood.

Genesis 38:20 And Judah sent the kid of the goats by the hand of his friend the Adullamite, to receive the pledge from the woman's hand: but he found her not.

38:21 Then he asked the men of her place, saying, Where is the harlot, that was at Enaim by the way side? And they said, There hath been no harlot here. (ESV)

As a pledge for payment, Judah gave her his signet, his cord, and his staff. When he sent his friend to pay the woman, she was gone. And not only was she not there, the people from that area said that there never was a harlot in that place. You have to wonder what kind of effect that must have had on Judah's mind. How could there never have been a harlot there? He gave those items to *somebody*.

So Tamar became pregnant by Judah. And when Judah learned that she was with child, he commanded to have her brought out and burned (not knowing that he himself was the father).

Gen 38:24 And it came to pass about three months after, that it was told Judah, saying, Tamar thy daughter in law hath played the harlot; and moreover, behold, she is with child by whoredom. And Judah said, Bring her forth, and let her be burnt.

38:25 When she was brought forth, she sent to her father in law, saying, By the man, whose these are, am I with child: and she said, Discern, I pray thee, whose are these, the signet, and the cords, and the staff.

38:26 And Judah acknowledged them, and said, She is more righteous than I; forasmuch as I gave her not to Shelah my son. And he knew her again no more. (ASV)

The struggle for Tamar was a struggle to bring forth seed. Both her husbands died and she was childless. The other son that was promised to her was withheld from her. So Tamar took the initiative, and claimed what was promised directly from the source of the promise: Judah. In doing so, she must have known that her life would hang in the balance. The pledge she took from Judah was her safeguard. We may question her tactics, but she laid down her life for the promised seed.

Genesis 38:27 And it came to pass in the time of her travail, that, behold, twins were in her womb.

38:28 And it came to pass, when she travailed, that the one put out his hand: and the midwife took and bound upon his hand a scarlet thread, saying, This came out first.

38:29 And it came to pass, as he drew back his hand, that, behold, his brother came out: and she said, How hast thou broken forth? this breach be upon thee: therefore his name was called Pharez.

Genesis 38:30 And afterward came out his brother, that had the scarlet thread upon his hand: and his name was called Zarah.

His name was called Pharez; because he *breached* his brother. Pharez means *breach*. Here we go again. His brother was named *Zarah*, which means, *rising*. The *rising* was *breached*. Another *"wall"* was broken, and the promised seed prevailed. And Tamar has her place in the genealogy of Jesus Christ.

Matthew 1:3 And Judah fathered Pharez and Zarah of Tamar. (MKJV)

And he saw also a certain poor widow….

Luke 21:2

Resources

Meyers, Rick, e-Sword® - The Sword of the LORD with an electronic edge, version 11.1.0 www.e-sword.net

This downloadable resource provided most of the Bible translations used in this work, to include word study resources as follows, which are public domain:

Brown-Driver-Briggs Hebrew Definitions
Greek Old Testament (Septuagint) w/ Stong's Numbers
Fausset's Bible Dictionary
Hitchcock's Bible Dictionary
Strong's Hebrew and Greek Dictionary

The following Internet resources were also used for Bible verse translations:

BibleGateway https://www.biblegateway.com/

Bible Hub https://biblehub.com/